THE NUCLEAR ARMS RACE:

COUNTDOWN TO DISASTER

A study in Christian ethics.

The Rev. William W. Rankin

**With an introduction by
The Rev. George F. Regas,
Convenor of the Arms Race Task Force
of the Episcopal Urban Caucus**

How To Use This Book

COUNTDOWN TO DISASTER is published as source material for group discussions. It also may be used for individual study and reflection.

At the end of each chapter are discussion questions that encourage a personal response to the material found in that chapter. With six chapters, the book lends itself, therefore, to at least six group sessions.

At the end of the book is the platform statement adopted by the Episcopal Urban Caucus in February, 1981. It includes a strategies statement and concludes with a special liturgy. This liturgy, using Rite Two from *The Book of Common Prayer,* is designed as the first step toward active peacemaking.

George F. Regas, who wrote the introduction to this book and The Forward Movement publication, *Reversing the Arms Race* (1980), has called arms reduction, "the quintessential task of the Church." Whether you agree or disagree, you are bound to find COUNTDOWN TO DISASTER one of the clearest analyses made of this crucial and complex subject.

Editor

The Arms Race Task Force of the Episcopal Urban Caucus

The Episcopal Urban Caucus came into being in 1980 in response to information gathered during hearings held by the Urban Bishops Coalition. The hearings revealed the agony and the anger, the discouragement and the despair, of the many poor people who inhabit our cities. It is the purpose of EUC to assist the Episcopal Church in directing its resources toward the needs of those voices heard at the hearings. The Arms Race Task Force of the EUC is charged with helping the Episcopal Church to understand and respond to the role of the arms race in these problems.

Contents

Credit

We are deeply grateful to Paul Conrad and *The Los Angeles Times* for permission to reprint the illustrations in this book. All are shown with copyright notice and year published.

©1981 Forward Movement Publications, 412 Sycamore Street, Cincinnati, Ohio 45202

INTRODUCTION

There is growing in America today a dangerous spirit of militarism which is coupled with a reckless neglect of our nation's cities. Against this backdrop, Jesus' words ring with new urgency for 20th Century people: "Blessed are the peacemakers, for they shall be called the children of God." In this study guide, Dr. William Rankin has written about the urgent need for faithful peacemaking.

The book presents the case that militarism is hurting most of us, especially those who are already suffering; namely, the poor and members of racial minorities. In the end, the arms race may kill us all unless we stop it.

As General Eisenhower pointed out, "Every gun made, every warship launched, every rocket fired, signifies a theft from those who hunger, and are not fed; those who are cold, and are not clothed." The author's viewpoint is that the rise of militarism and the inseparably related misery of the poor are wrong, so dreadfully wrong as to compel the strongest, most sustained protest of which we are capable.

Of course, readers may decide for themselves. And to decide about militarism, the cities, racism and poverty is to demand much of a reader. The issues are complex and controversial. Most of us see ourselves as both rational and fair minded, and we believe deeply in this self-perception. Therefore, an openness to the information and ideas in this study guide is presupposed.

The data concerning the arms race are sometimes hard to find, frequently difficult to understand, and always changing. The same is true of the plight of the cities and the poor. The author has documented key statements, carefully constructed the ethical and biblical foundations on which our urgent peacemaking is to be established, and provided penetrating questions at the end of each chapter so readers may continue their explorations as they choose. Although this study guide is of necessity a modest offering, readers may at least get a sense of the magnitude of what is happening, the direction in which we in America seem to be moving, and the possibilities for Christian discipleship.

Bill Rankin is eminently qualified to write this book.

He was employed by a major United States defense firm where he worked on military projects with engineers whom he liked and admired. They were good people, hard working and intelligent. The piercing questions raised in this study about the causes and effects of huge military spending are not in any respect judgments against military personnel or defense industry employees. Rather they are an attempt to stimulate all of us to see beyond the "everydayness" of our lives to the human misery that is so wholly rooted in the militarism of our day.

Recently Rankin was employed by a large social services department in children's welfare work. There he came to know not only bureaucratic waste and foul-ups, but also the system's effectiveness. He has known the poor, their homes, their diets, and their health care. He has known the angry, the proud, the courageous, the mean, the sick, the beautiful and the defeated. He has worked with poor people and their children in hospitals, foster homes, churches, courts and jails. He writes, "Of the hundreds of the poor with whom I have worked, not one ever owned a Cadillac or preferred to receive welfare. Poor women and men are like you and me — just people who don't like to be dependent upon charity. But that they happen to be poor, and live in poverty — constant, omnipresent, dictatorial poverty — is the problem. For some, racism is the problem, too. When racism and poverty both work against people, adults are robbed of their self-respect, children are robbed of their childhood and all find their lives diminished. Worst of all is the end of hope for the future. That is why racism and poverty are the strongest threats to the good news of Christ."

Bill Rankin's academic credentials are impressive. He has earned a Ph.D. in Ethics and an M.A. in Policy Sciences and Public Affairs from Duke University.

For many years he has been an Episcopal priest serving on the staff at All Saints Church in Pasadena, California. Here he has been instrumental in creating a community of peacemakers who have tough minds, gentle spirits and passionate hearts.

This study guide has been a collaborative effort with a number of people on the Arms Race Task Force of the Episcopal Urban Caucus: Judith Erb, James Downward, William Coats, Gary Hall and William Yon. For their help with this project, thanks are also due to many others; chiefly Lynne Carolla, Martha Cockburn, Martin Ewing, Janet Langford, Sue Loyd, Carol McCrary, Anne Sutherland, Harmon Smith and Sally, Amy and Rob Rankin. Paul Conrad of the *Los Angeles Times* graciously supplied the cartoons. But Bill Rankin is responsible for the final product, and I am deeply grateful for his offering to the peace of the world.

The world is now on, as George Kennen describes it, ". . . a countdown to disaster." In Morris West's provocative novel, *The Clowns of God,* a daughter says to her father, "You've given us everything except tomorrow. I don't want my baby to be born in a bomb shelter and die of radiation sickness." This book is dedicated to the children of the world in the daring hope that the peacemakers will have the last word.

George F. Regas
Convenor, Arms Race Task Force, Episcopal Urban Caucus

1.
THE NUCLEAR AGE

"O God, who art the author of peace and lover of concord, in knowledge of whom standeth our eternal life, whose service is perfect freedom: Defend us, thy humble servants, in all assaults of our enemies; that we, surely trusting in thy defense, may not fear the power of any adversaries; through the might of Jesus Christ our Lord."

The Book of Common Prayer, p. 57

This Collect for Peace identifies God as the source of peace, the only defense worthy of our ultimate trust. But, "some put their trust in horses," as the Psalms have it; horses being the military vehicles of ancient times.

In whom, then, is our trust? How practical is faith in God these days? It would be splendid if everyone lived by religious faith and moral principles; but since all do not, a certain realism is necessary. Only the naive believe in God's goodness alone, as if evil, "original sin," or ordinary human cussedness were not a factor in life as well.

Chapter 1 attempts to characterize today's nuclear arms race for persons who recognize that the world is indeed imperfect, and yet desire to live by Christian principles. Most people acknowledge that we live in an age qualitatively different from the pre-1945 era. Our first task as Christians is to get at least a sense of that era, the "nuclear era," while we seek to discern the spirit of God and what is required of us. Few Christians disagree that there is much to be done in the world; but which things are most important? The following material is intended to show that the nuclear arms race is sufficiently worrisome to warrant our urgent attention.

* * *

THE NUCLEAR AGE

The Experience

At 8:15 A.M. shops, offices, and businesses are alive with the ordinary activity of a city's life. Even schools are in session this August morning — at least for children who are not yet evacuated.

At 8:15 A.M. on August 6 a bell rings in the broadcasting department of NHK, the Japanese Broadcasting Corporation. A warning is received from the Chugoku District Army Headquarters, and the radio announcer begins to read the bulletin, "Chugoku District Army Information. Three enemy airplanes have been spotted over the Saijo area . . ." Suddenly there is an awesome roar, and the announcer is hurled into the air.

The people closest to the detonation point are suddenly evaporated; only their shadows remain. Those who can move are terribly burned. Their skin hangs off them in large strips as they run, sometimes stagger, towards the river banks.

It begins to rain: "black rain" — ash, radioactive fallout.

Endless lines of women, men, and children stream toward the outskirts of Hiroshima, or to its river edges, seeking water.

One year later the mayor, Mr. Hamai, reads the first Hiroshima "Peace Declaration." He says, "Those who have experienced and fully realized the anguish and sin of war would denounce war absolutely as the ultimate agony, and wish for peace most passionately."[1]

*

The mother sees her child dragging the step ladder to a place beneath the pomegranate tree. Her husband had bought the ladder before he was killed in the war.

Slowly the child climbs the ladder, finally reaches the ripe fruit. He nuzzles each one in turn and whispers, "Don't fall, pomegranate, till I come back again."[2]

There is a light blue flash, and a fireball 200 meters in diameter moves outward from the bomb's blast center. The temperature reaches 300,000°c. The pressure of the explosion nearest the detonation point ranges from 4.5 and 6.7 tons per square meter.

The child is no more.

The fires of Hiroshima burn for the next two days.

*

There is a river which runs through Hiroshima. Every year the descendents of the bomb victims set upon it floating lanterns containing the names of the family dead. For many miles the entire breadth of the river is one mass of flame.[3]

*

8

"At Hiroshima there's a museum, and outside that museum there's a rock, and on that rock there's a shadow. That shadow is all that remains of the human being who stood there on August 6, 1945 when the nuclear age began."[4]

The Prospect

It has been determined that a 20-megaton thermonuclear bomb exploded on a clear day at ground level on a large east-coast city would create a fireball one and a half miles in diameter, with temperatures of 20 million to 30 million degrees fahrenheit . . .

At 6 miles from the epicenter, all people would be instantly killed by a huge silent heat flash travelling at the speed of light . . .

A single nuclear device would result in hundreds of thousands of severe burn injuries. The entire U.S. has intensive care facilities for fewer than 2,000 such cases . . .

Fires from ignition of oil storage tanks, natural gas lines, gasoline and LNG tanks might coalesce into an enormous firestorm 1,200 square miles in area, fanned by 100-200 mile per hour winds, creating temperatures capable of cooking and asphyxiating those in shelters . . .[5]

Worldwide fallout would cause deaths, illnesses, and the possible destruction of the ozone layer, changes in the earth's temperature and mutilation of crops. It would be a different world afterwards, colder, harsher, and contaminated by radiation for thousands of years. The number of deaths would break scales of comparison.[6]

*

How shall we conceive of only *one* megaton? How much TNT would produce a blast equivalent to one megaton? If we transported by train one megaton's equivalent of TNT, the train would consist of boxcars in a line 300 miles long. If you were waiting at a railroad crossing for the train to pass, and if the train were moving at 50 miles per hour, you would watch TNT rush by for six hours.

Such explosive power is deliverable by a *single* Polaris missile to any location in the world.[7]

*

The U.S. Office of Technology Assessment has determined that a 1-megaton warhead detonated about 1 mile over Detroit would kill 470,000 persons instantly and severly injure, mostly by burns, another 630,000.

The same study notes that warheads exploding at ground level around the area of our missile silos would generate large clouds of radioactive dust and cause from 1 million to 20 million casualties among the civilian population.

9

In the United States, according to this study, an all-out nuclear war would kill 20 to 25 million, on the low side, to 155 to 165 million on the high side. If the relatively low figure described instant deaths, large numbers of persons would be expected to die more slowly over an extended period. The inability of whatever health care systems remained to function adequately would add to the problem. Political and economic structures of society would be severely damaged as well.[8]

The Preparation

As contrasted to land-based intercontinental missiles, a feature of nuclear missile submarines is their ability to carry weapons of enormous destructive force while remaining scattered and well hidden. Today the world's oceans conceal up to 5 U.S. Polaris submarines, 16 Poseidon submarines, and 6 Trident subs. To describe but one case, a single Poseidon missile submarine surfaces at some location in the thousands of miles of ocean water. It carries 16 missiles aimed at the Soviet Union. Resting on each missile are 10 to 14 nuclear warheads. Each warhead is independently targeted for a Soviet site. Each warhead can explode with 40 kilotons force, more than twice the explosive force that ripped Hiroshima and Nagasaki. *One* easily-concealed Poseidon submarine can today destroy *at least* 160 Soviet cities.[9]

*

According to *Chemical & Engineering News,* the U.S. has, ". . . about 9,000 strategic nuclear weapons that can be delivered from bases in the U.S. to targets in the Soviet Union or elsewhere with high reliability. The smallest of these strategic weapons has more than twice the explosive yield of the bombs dropped on Hiroshima and Nagaski. The largest is 600 times more powerful."[10]

*

We speak of "deterrence" as the ability to inflict unacceptable damage upon an adversary. The adversary recognizes that unacceptably destructive retaliation would follow from his first strike; therefore he is deterred from initiating an attack. The key to deterrence consists in determining the level of "unacceptable damage." Some believe that the ability of the U.S. to destroy Moscow is sufficient to deter a Soviet strike against our country. Others believe that our ability to destroy the five largest Soviet population centers constitutes a sufficient deterrence. Still others think that deterrence is possible only by the threat of massive destruction.

*

As distinguished from simple "deterrence," the arms race means the production and deployment of weapons in greater and greater numbers and destructive power so as to keep up with, or ahead of, an adversary. One matches, or tries to surpass, what the other has. This is the arms race. Currently, the U.S. possesses 2,152 nuclear warheads for strategic land-based missiles, while the Soviets possess 5,500. The Soviets are ahead in the land-based missile strategic nuclear warhead race. But the U.S. possesses 4,880 submarine launched strategic ballistic missile warheads, whereas the Soviets own only 1,334 of these. The U.S. leads in the submarine missile area. The U.S. owns 1,926 nuclear warheads deliverable from strategic bombers, as opposed to only 260 of these for the Soviets. Here, also, the U.S. is ahead. Finally, the U.S. owns 1,500 nuclear warheads capable of delivery to the Soviet Union from European bases or aircraft carriers. The Soviets have no corresponding capability.[11]

If one believes that one Poseidon submarine's ability to destroy 160 Soviet cities is sufficient to deter the Soviets from nuclear war, then there would be about 10,000 extraneous nuclear warheads, strategic and tactical, in the current U.S. arsenal. These 10,000 extra nuclear warheads are one way to think of the difference between "deterring" and "racing" the Soviet Union.

*

The newest generation of U.S. weapons, the so-called "counterforce" weapons, are characterized by remarkable accuracy, including the ability to hit enemy missile silos, and the destructive force that we associate with any nuclear warhead. These weapons include the MX, Trident II, and Cruise missiles.

Critics believe that counterforce weapons are dangerous because, 1) they give the adversary an incentive to strike first (empty his silos), 2) they also give *us* the incentive to strike first, as we will see, and, 3) they encourage the other side to get the same sort of weapons, increasing uncertainty all around.

Supporters say that counterforce weapons are essential to the U.S. arsenal because, sooner or later, they will become part of the Soviet arsenal. They believe, too, that any qualitative improvements in weaponry are good, per se. According to Presidential Directive 59, released in August 1980, the chief rationale for the Counterforce strategy is that U.S. nuclear weapons are now targeted more "flexibly" at Soviet military rather than civilian population centers and industrial targets. But a severe difficulty with all this is the notion that small nuclear wars can occur with the U.S. and Soviets attacking *only* each other's weapons installations. The "unthinkable" begins to become "thinkable."

Proliferation

There are presently five nations known to have nuclear weapons and the ability to deliver them to an enemy target: the United States, the Soviet Union, China, the United Kingdom, and France. It has been noted that today the "production of sufficient fissile material for a modest nuclear force is within the reach of virtually any country that decides to do so, on a small scale and secretly, once a nuclear reactor has been acquired specifically for this purpose."[12] Today Argentina, India, Pakistan, Brazil, Iran, Egypt, Israel, South Korea, South Africa, Mexico, Iraq, and Taiwan have or are constructing such nuclear reactors. India has already detonated a nuclear weapon, though she may not yet have a delivery system for it. Some believe that Israel possesses nuclear weapons, though this remains a conjecture thus far. Cuba and Libya have stated their intentions to explore nuclear possibilities. The prestigious Stockholm International Peace Research Institute (SIPRI) estimates that there may be 35 nations in the nuclear club by 1985.[13] The chances of someone's setting off a nuclear war seem to be increasing at an impressive rate.

Containment of Communism

It is frequently argued that the United States is, or ought to be, in competition with the Soviet Union for influence in Third World countries. Implicit in many such views is the notion that influence is best obtained by supplying arms to foreign governments, rather than, say, supplying civilian aid to their citizenry. The warrant for this strategy is that it effectively opposes the spread of communism. *The deeper question, to be considered shortly, is: how did the assumption that the best interests of the United States equates with the containment of communism become an accepted premise of American life?*

There has been no lack of alarm over Soviet designs on Third World countries. Attention has recently focused upon Angola (where Cuban soldiers were stationed), Ethiopia, Iran, and particularly Afghanistan. Certainly the Soviets may be expected to desire the friendship of Third World governments, (but those countries have not always responded in kindness). The continuing reports from Afghanistan, for example, indicate deep and widespread resistance to the Soviet presence in that country. Indeed, some observers see parallels between the costly Soviet adventure in Afghanistan and the terribly difficult involvement of the United States in Southeast Asia. (To give yet another example, the recent events in Iran have the marks only of internal power struggles, with no significant evidence of Soviet influence at all.)

Sometimes one nation's bellicosity is symptomatic of fear. Soviet denunciation of U.S. "imperialism" may be an expression of innate Soviet belligerence, as some believe; but more persuasive is the view that the Soviets are sincerely worried about what they perceive as U.S. hostility toward them. U.S. resolve to stop communism in many countries around the world is the subject of much official policy in this country, and the policy has often been backed by commitments of money, weapons, and even personnel. Whether this is right or wrong is not pertinent to our present purpose; what is important is to recognize that the Soviets have been given reason to worry about U.S. anti-Soviet sentiment.

Since the frequent U.S. military involvements in Third World countries since World War II have been announced as "anti-Soviet" in intention, and sometimes with controversial results, it is important to understand the recent origin of this tendency. We might begin with the influential book, *The Uncertain Trumpet*,[14] written by General Maxwell Taylor, an Army Chief of Staff during the Eisenhower years. In his book General Taylor argued for a greater U.S. emphasis upon the development of conventional arms. He envisioned increased U.S. military involvement in Third World countries as a way to block communist influence there. Taylor certainly did not intend to nourish U.S.-Soviet nuclear conflicts in Third World countries, but two decades later, with the expanding availability of nuclear weapons, his thesis is much more dangerous than when he himself first presented it. His book, in any case, was motivated by a desire to recover the slipping prestige of the army, whose budget was dwindling in contrast to that of the air force. This reflected the contemporary enthusiasm over nuclear weapons and a recognition of the air force's ability to deliver them.

For Taylor, the army's value included its ability to fight conventional wars in Third World countries. Latin America had always been seen as a legitimate area for U.S. involvement, but a case needed to be made for military involvement in Asia, Africa, and the Middle East. Taylor's theory was that these areas were essentially testing grounds for U.S. or Soviet influence, and that political changes in them added to the advantage of one superpower while diminishing the influence of the other. Thus any change in the internal affairs of a Third World country had a deeper significance, according to Taylor, in terms of the U.S. cold war struggle against the Soviet Union. That Taylor's thesis was not correct with regard to many specific situations did not diminish its effectiveness as a general design for foreign policy.

The predisposition to view Third World conflicts as significant in terms of U.S. versus Soviet conflict has been challenged by many, perhaps most forcibly by Arthur Schlesinger, Jr. Writing in the *Wall*

Street Journal,[15] Schlesinger asserts that the tendency to view Third World conflicts in terms of a Soviet conspiracy and cold war theory is "hopelessly erroneous." He states, "There was unrest in the world long before there was a Bolshevik Revolution; there will be unrest long after Brezhnev and his gang are forgotten." Schlesinger continues, "If the Soviet Union did not exist, Iraq and Iran would still be at war; Israelis and Palestinians would still be at each other's throats; there would still be no peace in Northern Ireland, Cambodia or South Africa — and there would still be civil war in El Salvador." He adds that ancient animosities, religious feuds, class antagonisms and other factors existed long before the U.S.-Soviet rivalry, and that these local factors are the driving force of Third World unrest. With the proliferation of nuclear weapons, a new element is added to the mix of Third World tensions. The dangers posed by such weapons make advisable the re-evaluation of U.S. rationales for military involvement in the Third World. Third World hostilities have always held the danger of expanding to regional, then global, levels. To see them in principle as part of a U.S.-Soviet conflict is, in the nuclear age, quite dangerous.

Nuclear Spread and Moral Thicket

Apart from other considerations, there are frequently moral factors of significance involved in the potential nuclear capabilities of certain nations. South Africa, with its official policies of racial exclusion, is perhaps the most obvious case in point. The support of Western nations to the South African nuclear effort began as early as the late 1940s when the Combined Development Agency was formed by the U.S. and Great Britain to find and develop South African uranium deposits.

In 1957 the U.S.-based Allis Chalmers company agreed to build the first South African nuclear research reactor, the Safari I. This was accomplished in 1961. By the same agreement, over 150 South African nuclear scientists and engineers have received training in the U.S. More recently, the Westinghouse Corporation, through its participation in a French consortium headed by Framatome, has provided the design for two nuclear power reactors presently under construction at Koeberg in South Africa.[16]

The increasing isolation of South Africa's government from enlightened world opinion, and from her immediate neighbors to the north, coupled with the effects of that nation's cruel policies upon her black and "coloured" populations, makes for an increasingly tense situation. A number of observers of South Africa are on record as believing that the situation there is explosive. That the primary source of arms for South Africa is the United States, and that the primary arms supplier to the black, anti-apartheid, African National Congress is the Soviet Union, makes the potential explosiveness of the situation even more alarming. It is within this context that two recent events take on a peculiar significance.

In August of 1977 both Soviet and U.S. surveillance satellites observed preparations in the Kalahari Desert to detonate a nuclear device. The South African government yielded to pressure from the U.S., France, and Great Britain not to carry out the test.

On September 22, 1979, a U.S. Vela satellite registered what appeared to be a nuclear explosion off South Africa's coast in the South Atlantic Ocean. President Carter appointed a panel of experts to review the Vela data to determine whether a nuclear blast had occurred. After nine months the government panel reported its belief that the satellite was probably hit by a meteorite which caused it to report mistakenly. These findings were strongly contested by a 300-page Naval Research Report, and by scientists at the Los Alamos nuclear weapons laboratory, both groups asserting that Vela had accurately reported a nuclear explosion.

Since South Africa's Deputy Defense Minister Hendrik Coetsee has told *Newsweek,* "If nuclear weapons are a last resort to defend oneself, it would be very stupid not to use them," it is not too difficult to imagine a disaster of major proportions emerging in that country.[17] The moral questions associated with using nuclear weapons would be compounded by their use against an oppressed racial majority.

But apart from the South Africa case, other moral problems are evident when one considers military spending impacts upon non-aligned countries worldwide. It should not seem surprising that according to the prestigious Brandt Commission, worldwide military spending approaches 450 billion U.S. dollars, while a number of problems facing poor countries are not being met when, in principle at least, they could be met. The Brandt Commission report notes that "The (worldwide) military expenditure of only half a day would suffice to finance the whole malaria eradication programme of the World Health Organization, and less would be needed to conquer river-blindness, which is still the scourge of millions."[18] For the price of one modern tank, 1,000 classrooms could be provided for 30,000 children in the developing countries. For the cost of one jet fighter, 40,000 village pharmacies could be established in poor countries.

In consideration of these trade-offs, *Disarmament and World Development* concludes, "Many of the major problems faced by the world community, problems of development, economic imbalance and inflation, pollution, energy and raw materials, trade relations and technology, and so forth, are enhanced and exacerbated by the arms race. Progress in other areas such as health, education, housing and many more is delayed owing to lack of resources . . . Against this background of a darkened economic outlook and a greater awareness of the scarcity of resources and the fragility of the physical environment, the continued mindless and uninhibited wastage of the arms race becomes ever more incongruous and unacceptable."[19]

Even as early as 1976, total military expenditure worldwide surpassed the *combined* Gross National Product of South Asia, the Far East, and Africa. Five years ago world military expenditures reached approximately $1 billion per day, or about $40 million per hour.[20]

Willem Boichel of the Society for International Development writes of the "historic discontinuity" with which all humanity is faced. He notes the "astonishing and truly horrific" explosive power equivalent to 50 million tons of TNT in the world. He writes also that more than a quarter of the human species live in degraded squalor. Elementary needs remain unmet in the areas of food, health, trade, education, housing, clothing, and employment.[21] The ways in which malnutrition, poor health, poor education, and fertility combine to express and reinforce poverty are admirably stated in a number of excellent studies, one of the best being the World Bank's *World Development Report, 1980.*[22] This report substantiates the evidence from a wide number of sources that gains in "human development" (what we might call the overall population quality) are desirable not only from a humanitarian but also from an economic development point of view. The conditions of "absolute poverty" in which 800 million people exist are all too grim and all too familiar to Christians who have kept abreast of church missionary and relief efforts. That three-quarters of a billion people, in the World Bank's words, "have barely enough income to keep themselves alive from week to week," constitutes an enormous challenge to the Christian community worldwide.

The moral dimension of military spending in the face of such widespread and abject poverty is presented by Arthur Simon of the Church organization Bread for the World. In his 1975 book Simon reports that each billion dollars now spent on the arms race represents "600 additional calories and 20 additional grams of protein" that could be used to help feed "50 million of the world's undernourished children for a year." Again, using figures available in 1975, Simon notes that U.S. military spending alone is about seven times the entire national budget of India. More, U.S. military spending alone is greater than the combined incomes of earth's poorest billion people. And U.S. daily military spending far surpasses the annual World Food Program budget of the United Nations, while it approximates the annual spending of the United

Nations Development program.[23] One need only recall the bloated bellies of children to be aware that "guns or butter" means most basically "death or life" to millions of God's precious ones. The arms race, then, has the property of contributing to the slow deaths of millions in the poorest countries of the world; while nuclear arms proliferation to tense, insecure, perhaps desperate, Third World governments also threatens to bring on the instantaneous deaths of millions in the final apocalypse.

Pope Paul VI, mindful of the opportunities foregone in human development as billions are spent on weapons, put the matter most succinctly: "The arms race kills without firing a shot."

Willem Boichel sums up. "The human family must ask itself the profound question: *WHY?* Why the fatal order of priorities and why is technology not being preponderantly used to improve the welfare of humanity?" Though Boichel finds the answers to his question in the "inherited social and economic structures" and the "value-laden ideologies" of the past, he hopes for the emergence in the future of new ". . . values and attitudes which will foster planetary solidarity, collective morality and universal ecological awareness." Indeed, ". . . either mankind cries out its opinion that common values, needs and aspirations take total and absolute precedence over the arms race, or humanity remains silent and beckons the forces of certain mass annihilation."[24]

1. *Unforgettable Fire: Pictures Drawn by Atomic Bomb Survivors.* Edited by the Japanese Broadcasting Corporation. New York: ©Pantheon Books, a division of Random House. 1977. (111 pp.) p. 9. Used by permission.

2. Masuji Ibuse, *Black Rain.* Tokyo, New York and San Francisco: Kodansha International Ltd. 1969. Translated by John Bester. (300 pp.) p. 123.

3. *Protest and Survive.* Edited by E. P. Thompson and Dan Smith. New York: Penguin Books. 1980. (264 pp.) p. 33.

4. Sydney Lens, "Mobilizing for Survival," *Washington Watch.* Vol. 5, No. 47, December 2, 1977. Lansing, Michigan.

5. *What is the Physician's Role in Preventing a Nuclear War?,* by Physicians for Social Responsibility. Watertown, Mass. 1979. (pamphlet)

6. *Ibid.*

7. J. Robert Nelson, "Scientists Preach Peace at MIT," *The Christian Century.* August 15-22, 1979. p. 779.

8. Reprinted with permission from *Chemical and Engineering News.* March 16, 1981. p. 26. ©1981 American Chemical Society.

9. Robert C. Aldridge, *The Counterforce Syndrome: A Guide to U.S. Nuclear Weapons & Strategic Doctrine.* Washington: Institute for Policy Studies. 1978. (86 pp.) p. 10. A Trident Submarine reportedly could destroy 240 cities.

10. *Chemical and Engineering News,* March 16, 1981. p. 26. See above.

11. *Ibid.*

12. Jolby, Richard, ed., *Disarmament & World Development.* Oxford: Pergamon Press. 1978. Used by permission.

13. Barnaby, Frank, "The Mounting Prospects of Nuclear War — A Report of the Stockholm International Peace Research Institute," *The Bulletin of the Atomic Scientists.* June, 1977, The Case of Pakistan, to cite but one example, is described in "Nuclear Curry," *Wall Street Journal,* May 11, 1981.

14. Taylor, Maxwell, *The Uncertain Trumpet.* New York: Harper & Row. 1960.

15. Schlesinger, Arthur, Jr., "The Soviet Conspiracy and World Unrest," *Wall Street Journal,* February 23, 1981.

16. A detailed treatment of international corporate involvement in South African nuclear weapons development is given by Raimo Vayrynen in "The Role of Transnational Corporations in the Military Sector of South Africa," *Journal of Southern African Affairs.* Vol. 5: No. 2. April 1980. pp. 199-255.

17. Coetsee's quote appears in *Southern Africa,* Vol. XIV: No. 1. January/February 1981. p. 22.

18. *North-South: A Program for Survival.* Cambridge: The MIT Press. 1980. p. 14. Used by permission.

19. Jolby, *ibid.*

20. Boichel, Willem, "Accelerated Nuclear and Conventional Militarization of the World Cripples Development, Undermines Global Restructuring Efforts and Increases Probability of Nuclear Armageddon." *Survey of International Development.* Vol. XV: Nos. 2 & 3. March/June 1978. p. 2.

21. Boichel, *ibid.*

22. World Bank, *World Development Report, 1980.* Washington, D.C. August 1980. 165 pp.

23. Simon, Arthur, *Bread for the World.* New York: Paulist Press. p. 123.

24. Boichel, *ibid.,* p. 6.

DISCUSSION QUESTIONS:
CHAPTER ONE:
THE NUCLEAR AGE

1. August 6, 1945 — Hiroshima — The Feast of the Transfiguration — the transfiguration of power, when, as Einstein said, "everything changed except our way of thinking." Do we learn from history? What did we learn? Did different people learn different things, depending upon where they were on August 6, 1945?

2. August 6, 1982. Radio and television broadcasting is interrupted. The President is about to deliver an urgent message to the nation. What do you imagine he will say? Do you feel secure?

3. In consideration of the projected results of one 20-megaton thermonuclear bomb blast, what does it mean to *win* a nuclear war?

4. If the other side launched a nuclear attack against the U.S., what should the U.S. do? Why?

5. In an arms race of such destructive potential, what does arms "superiority" mean?

6. What is the difference between "deterrence" and "arms race"? Should the difference in concepts have significance for foreign policy? For military spending?

7. Suppose you were a policy analyst asked to submit to the President a policy concerning Counterforce weapons: Whether to build them or not. What would you recommend? Why?

8. Suppose you were to give an address to your church school class on the topic "Jesus Christ and the development of nuclear weapons." What major themes would you touch upon in your talk? Why?

9. Evaluate the proposition that the containment of communism is always in the best interest of the United States.

10. What are the benefits and risks of the spread of nuclear technology to other countries? Who benefits? Who is at risk? Why?

11. What is your view of U.S.-Soviet competition in the Third World? What kinds of policies should govern U.S. Anti-Soviet activities in the Third World? Why?

12. What are the moral issues regarding large military spending in the face of poverty in the poorest countries?

13. Can you remember where you were and what you thought when various major events occurred, such as the bombing of Pearl Harbor, the bombing of Hiroshima, the testing of nuclear weapons by the Soviets, and the like? What impacts did these events have upon your life?

2.

NUCLEAR WEAPONS

"As Christians, we recognize a demonic element in the complexity of
our world, but we also affirm our belief in the good will and purpose and
Providence of God for his whole creation. This requires us to work for a
world characterized not by fear, but by mutual trust and justice.

"Mankind is confronted with a choice: we must halt the arms race and
proceed to disarmament, or face annihilation."

The Primates of the worldwide
Anglican Church, Washington, D.C. 1981

Our spiritual struggle includes the recognition that the Christ bids us to
trust in him, his Kingdom, the new creation; yet we prepare for war, as if
the powers of the old age are determinative of our choices and our
conduct.

What does it mean really to trust spiritually in the dominance of good,
when materially we "prepare for the worst"?

What kinds of suffering are we prepared to endure in trusting the good?
What kinds of suffering are we preparing to inflict in fearing the evil?

If our souls confront the Christ, our bodies confront the Soviets. With
our hands and minds we have fashioned a national security that does not
make us *feel* as secure as we would prefer.

To seek security is one of the most basic of all religious impulses. But
have we sought our security in the right place? By the right means? In
seeking security have we found God? Or something else?

The present chapter portrays the various weapons available to make us
secure. It also offers comparisons with Soviet weapons, to enable an
informed judgment concerning the degree and kind of security we have.
We may be able to see by careful study of this chapter what we have
wrought. Along the way, with the support of our sisters and brothers and
God's Holy Spirit, we may ask, is this what we want?

* * *

"...MX...BOMBERS...BATTLESHIPS...FIGHTERS...
NEUTRON BOMBS...MISSILES...NUCLEAR SUBS...
TANKS...AUTOMATIC WEAPONS...THE TRULY NEEDY..."

23

NUCLEAR WEAPONS

Current U.S. and Soviet Military Capabilities

The United States strategic nuclear weapon strategy consists in a three-part structure (the "TRIAD") comprised of land-based Intercontinental Ballistic Missiles (ICBMs), Submarine Launched Ballistic Missiles (SLBMs), and long-range bombers. The U.S. has sought to maintain an even balance between each of the three components. The USSR, on the other hand, has placed more emphasis upon their ICBM force, only recently giving more attention to their SLBM capability, and currently lagging far behind the U.S. in bombers.

In general, "strategic" weapons are those which can be launched from within a country and be expected to penetrate deeply into an adversary's territory. These are long-range weapons. "Tactical weapons," sometimes called "theater" weapons, are of shorter-range, and are deployed by the U.S. and its NATO allies in Europe. The Soviet Union and its Warsaw Pact allies have also deployed what the U.S. calls "tactical" weapons (nuclear and conventional) in Europe.

The following data are drawn from Defense Department publications, chiefly the *Report of Secretary of Defense Harold Brown to the Congress on the FY 1982 Budget, FY 1983 Authorization Request and FY 1982-86 Defense Programs.* (Washington, D.C., January 19, 1981. 317 pp.)

Land-based ICBMs:
The nature of the United States ICBM capability can be seen by the following table:

No.	Name	First Deployed	Warheads Per Missile	Warhead Yield (Megatons)	Accuracy (C. E. P.)*	Range (Mi.)
52	Titan II	1963	1	9	.80	7,500
450	Minuteman II	1965	1	1-2	.35	8,000
250	Minuteman III	1970	3 (MIRV)	.175	.20	7,500
300	Minuteman III (modified)	1981	3 (MIRV)	.335	.10	8,000

*C.E.P.: half the missiles will land within this distance from target.

The Titan II missiles are eventually to be replaced, since as liquid fuel missiles they are difficult to maintain. The other missiles are solid fuel types, hence are much more easily maintained. Moreover the relatively high C.E.P.[1] of .80 means that the Titan IIs are particularly inaccurate. The warhead yield of 9 megatons for each Titan II missile is the

24

equivalent of three times the total bombing tonnage of World War II.

The Minuteman III and III (modified) missiles contain MIRV (Multiple-Independently-targeted Re-entry Vehicles) warheads. This means that the three warheads on the tip of each Minuteman III missile can be aimed at separate targets. The missile's job is to get the three warheads into the general target locations. In the case of the modified Minuteman III, the low C.E.P. means a very high degree of accuracy — due to the Mark 12A warheads, which can deliver a nuclear device to within 600 feet of its target.

The Soviet Union's ICBM capability, which is the major part of its entire nuclear defense structure, is as follows:

Name	No. Deployed	Warheads Per Missile	Warhead Yield (Megatons)	Accuracy (C. E. P.)	Range (Mi.)	First Deployed
SS-11	500	1	.95	.75	6,000	1966
SS-13	60	?	?	?	?	?
SS-17	150	4	.75	.30	6,000	1975
		1	6	.30	6,000	1977
SS-18	300	1	24	.20	6,000	1974
(4 Mods)		10	.5	.10	5,500	1980?
SS-19	300	6	.55	.20	5,000	1974
		1	10	.20	5,500	1978

The SS-11 is as inaccurate as the U.S. Titan II missiles. The SS-13 is the only solid fuel missile in the entire Soviet array of ICBMs. That it has not been duplicated in subsequent versions seems to mean that the Soviets have simply failed so far to master solid fuel technology. The liquid fuel missiles that dominate the ICBM array are decidedly more difficult to maintain than solid fuel missiles would be. The SS-18 (modified) is the largest and most worrisome weapon to U.S. strategists. This is because of the ability of this missile to carry at least 10, and perhaps as many as 30, MIRV'd warheads and attack U.S. Minuteman missiles still in their silos.

On balance, the U.S. ICBM arsenal is impressive for its technological superiority over the Soviet ICBM systems. This is reflected in the solid fuel features, the longer range capabilities, and the remarkable accuracy of the Mark 12A warhead. The Soviet ICBMs are strong in their ability to deliver multiple warheads, and warheads of high megaton yield, though their range, accuracy and overall reliability are inferior to U.S. missiles.

Submarine Launched Ballistic Missiles (SLBMs):
The U.S. SLBM force consists in the following:

No. Subs	Name	First Deployed	Warheads Per Missile	Yield Per Warhead (Megatons)	Accuracy (C. E. P.)	Range (Mi.)
3 Polaris	A-3	1964	3	.20	.50	2,500
25 Poseidon	C-3	1971	10-14 (MIRV)	.04	.30	2,800
6 Poseidon	D-4					
10 Trident I	D-4	1979	10	.10	.20	4,000

The present Polaris fleet consists of 5 submarines, each carrying 16 missiles. The 3 warheads per missile are not independently targeted, but rather are intended to land in a brace around the same target. These subs are destined for future replacement by the more accurate and powerful Tridents.

The Poseidon fleet consists of 31 submarines, each carrying 16 missiles. The 7 to 10 warheads per missile are all independently targeted. The planned fleet of 10 Trident I subs, each having a capacity of 24 missiles, also has 10 MIRV'd warheads per missile, and a missile range of 4,000 miles.

The Soviet capability looks like this:

No. Subs	Missile Desig.	First Deployed	Warheads Per Missile	Yield Per Warhead (Megatons)	Accuracy (C. E. P.)	Range (Mi.)
29 Yankee	SS-N-6	1968	1	.50	.70	1,600
20 Delta I-II	SS-N-8	1973	1	.05-1.0	.80	4,800
10 Delta III	SS-N-18	1977	3	1.0	.80	4,800

The Soviet Yankee is thought by most people to be inferior to the U.S. Polaris submarine. The Soviets have 29 of these subs, each carrying a dozen missiles. The Delta I and II submarines carry about a dozen missiles, and there are about 20 of these subs. The Soviets have at least ten Delta III submarines, with about 12 missiles per sub.

On balance, the accuracy of U.S. SLBMs, and the overwhelming number of warheads deliverable by U.S. subs, place the U.S. at a distinct advantage over the Soviets in the submarine area. The superior technology invested in U.S. subs makes them decidedly less vulnerable to detection, refueling, and other maintenance and operational factors than is the case with Soviet submarines.

Bombers:

The United States possesses 350 B-52 bombers, which are subsonic, essentially older aircraft, but with continuously upgraded electronic systems of various sorts. These planes can penetrate deep into an adversary's territory at low altitude, giving them good protection from radar detection. Each plane can carry four large nuclear bombs.

The Soviet long range bomber forces consist of 49 Bison and 100 Bear bombers. Each of these, like the B-52, is subsonic, and neither is upgraded to the extent of the B-52. Another 70 Backfire bombers, subsonic, for "peripheral attack and naval missions" (according to the 1981 report issued by Secretary of Defense Weinberger) are in the Soviet air arsenal.

The U.S. has a considerable lead over the U.S.S.R. in the strategic bomber area, both in quality and quantity of bombers.

Readiness:

The United States keeps *all* its ICBMs at constant readiness, meaning that each missile can be launched within minutes. Further, 60% of U.S. missile-carrying subs are at sea at any given moment, and always one-third of the U.S. bomber force is on alert, able to fly upon 5 minutes' notice.

The U.S.S.R.'s land-based missiles are in a state of readiness unknown to us at the present time, because of our inability to get clear information. Only 15% of the Soviet missile subs are at sea at any given time, however, and Soviet bombers are not on "short alert" at all. Therefore the United States at any moment is more prepared for nuclear war than is the Soviet Union.

Grand Totals:

U.S.		U.S.S.R.
2,152	ICBM warheads	5,500
4,880	SLBM warheads	1,334
1,926	Bombers or short range air to surface missiles	260
8,958	Total force loadings	7,094

Very similar figures are given by the Defense Department for 1981 *(Annual Report: Fiscal Year 1982).* Defense Secretary Brown shows the U.S. possessing 9,000 "force loadings" in 1981 to 7,000 for the U.S.S.R. ("Force loadings", according to Brown, "reflect those independently-targetable weapons associated with the total operational ICBMs, SLBMs, and long range bombers.")[2]

To the U.S. total must be added at least 1,000 Tactical Nuclear Weapons (TNWs) in Europe, which can be delivered via FB111 and F-4 aircraft. The Soviets have no forward-based weapons able to reach the U.S.

The explosive force for both the U.S. and the U.S.S.R. balances out at approximately 10,000 megatons each, which is the equivalent explosive force of 10 billion tons of TNT, or 2.5 tons of TNT per person in the world. At the very least, the figures do not support those who assert that the Soviets have surpassed the United States in nuclear capability. It is more accurate to say that at least the United States and the Soviets are at parity.

Concerning the Future

Mr. Reagan, during his Presidential campaign, called for a "margin of safety" in the strategic nuclear arms competition with the Soviet Union. This "margin of safety" is apparently to be achieved by a nuclear arms escalation in quality and quantity significantly beyond the present Soviet capability. Such an endeavor would be assisted by spending 25% more money in the military sector in 1982 than was spent in 1981. This strategy reflects the President's preference for thinking in terms of superiority over the Soviets in an "arms race", rather than in terms of simple "deterrence."

To understand the idea of superiority, we can recall the recent history of the arms race. In the 1950's the U.S. possessed clear weapons superiority over the Soviets because of our medium and long-range bomber force. The Soviets resolved to match this force. The 1960's saw the U.S. leap ahead in a new way, this time by deploying ICBMs and missile-carrying submarines. Soviet technology at this point seemed about five years behind U.S. technology, but the Soviets committed themselves to ICBM and SLBM systems development. In 1970 the U.S. owned about 4,000 strategic nuclear warheads and bombs, to the Soviet Union's 1,800. During the decade of the 1970s the U.S. jumped ahead of the Soviet Union, again with a 5-year technological advantage, by developing MIRV'd warheads for both the Minuteman III and Poseidon missiles. The Soviets responded by developing MIRVs of their own. Today the U.S.S.R. has about 7,100 strategic warheads and bombs (a gain of 5,300 during the past decade), and the U.S. possesses about 9,000 strategic warheads and bombs (a gain of 5,000 since 1970). The Soviet determination to remain competitive with the U.S. seems indisputably a matter of record. Clear and lasting weapons superiority over them has never been achieved, though costs rise and stockpiles proliferate.

Presently official U.S. thinking continues the superiority logic of the arms race (again, as opposed to deterrence, say, in the form of a handful of nuclear warhead carrying submarines). This way of thinking lies at the heart of the so-called "worst case scenario."

The Worst Case Scenario

The "worst case scenario" has had the effect of mobilizing support for increased military spending and continued research and development of more advanced weapons systems. This seems understandable when we recall that political leaders charged with protecting and defending the people of the United States would be especially attentive to "what really worries" experts in military preparedness. Skeptics of "worst case scenarios," however, believe that commitments, policies, and priorities, which *as a rule* proceed from the worst possible condition, predispose the arms race to the most radical and rapid escalations. That is, the "worst case" approach in U.S. military planning tends, in the view of some, to become the "most likely case" — this because the Soviets are then forced to respond to U.S. preparations for the "worst case." The self-fulfilling nature of things tends to occur in a succession of "worst case" responses and counter-responses. The arms race escalates at an unnecessarily rapid rate according to this view.

Here is a typical Defense Department "worst case scenario."

Act I: The Soviets fire a "limited first strike" at the 1,052 Titan and Minuteman silos, using 2 warheads per silo to attain a high probability of success. Soviet submarines would simultaneously destroy the 40% of U.S. missile submarines not at sea at the moment, and the 60% of U.S. bombers not on alert. 10 million U.S. civilians would die.

Act II: The U.S. President decides either to do nothing to retaliate, or he chooses to fire the operational, surviving missiles and bombs, causing 100 million instant deaths in the Soviet Union.

Act III: If the U.S. retaliates, the Soviet Union launches its remaining 3,000 or so ICBMs and 1,000 or so SLBMs. There would be 100 million instant deaths in the U.S.

Having posed the "worst case scenario," the military planners go on to suggest a way to prevent the worst case from occurring. The solution is to deploy highly accurate, high-yield weapons ("counterforce" weapons) capable of destroying Soviet missiles in their silos. But though the military contends only that counterforce weapons are just that — "useful against any force concentration" — to destroy enemy missiles in their silos obviously requires that *we* shoot *first!* Thus the logic of "counterforce" elides into "first strike," and the dangers of "first strike" — by either side — are spectacular.

The Counterforce Weapons

The new generation of "counterforce" weapons can be evaluated in light of the following data:

No.	Name	Proposed for Deployment	Warheads Per Missile	Warhead Yield (Megatons)	Accuracy (C. E. P.)	Range (Mi.)
100-200	MX	1986	10	.335	.05	7,500
10	Trident II, D-5	1989	7	.335	.05	6,000

Although current plans to deploy the MX are unclear, a familiar proposal is to place 200 MX missiles on mobile carriers and shuttle them throughout a 10,000 mile road system through 20,000 to 40,000 square miles of publicly-owned land in Utah and Nevada. Each of the 200 missiles would carry 10 warheads. Each warhead would be 26 times more powerful than the Hiroshima bomb. In its present form, that is with the planned 4,600 shelters rather than the 10,000 shelters to which the systems could be expanded, the cost lies somewhere between $50 billion and $100 billion. MX-advocates believe that the missile system will be a suitable future replacement for older ICBMs since the MX could be easily hidden. Critics aren't persuaded, as evidenced below.

The assumptions underlying the development of counterforce weapons seem to be the following.

Assumption #1: The Soviets might try to destroy U.S. ICBMs in their silos. Is it so? Some experts believe that it is impossible for *either* the U.S. *or* the Soviets to place a nuclear warhead within 600 feet of a hardened silo after a 6,000 mile flight — particularly when neither adversary has ever tested its guidance systems over the route they would follow in a war. The U.S. tests its missiles in an east-to-west fashion, firing them from California's Vandenburg Air Force base into the South Pacific. The Soviet Union tests its missiles in a west-to-east trajectory, from northern European Russia to the northern Pacific. The wartime, northern trajectory's gravitational, atmospheric and weather factors are largely unknown.

Additional complications are that for U.S. missiles to be destroyed the incoming Soviet missiles would have to be undetected in flight, would have to land virtually simultaneously, and would have to avoid the "fratricide" of one incoming warhead accidentally pre-detonating another incoming warhead aimed at the same target.

Assumption #2: The Soviet Union might think it in their self-interest to start a nuclear war. Why? How? It might be supposed that *every* U.S.

submarine not at sea, *every* bomber not on alert, and that *every* missile silo were knocked out; yet just *one* Trident submarine could still destroy the 240 largest population centers in the Soviet Union. Even if nothing were left of the people and resources of the U.S., and all that remained of North America were a radioactive wasteland, the annihilation of the 240 largest population centers of the Soviet Union would still be an enormous loss to the Soviets.

Assumption #3: The MX, or other counterforce weapons able to hit Soviet missile silos, adds to our feeling of insecurity. It is possible that an adversary, believing that incoming missiles have the accuracy and power to destroy its own missiles, would not wait for the incoming missiles to arrive. The adversary would have a plan to fire its missiles upon first discovering that incoming missiles were en route. This is the "launch upon warning" strategy, whereby satellite or radar detection of incoming missiles is fed to a computer which launches our missiles before theirs arrive to destroy them. The argument for programming a computer to "launch upon warning" is that, due to the adversary's ability to destroy our missiles, there is an urgent need to empty our silos. Hence there is not time enough for a human decision to be made; i.e., for information to be assembled, for an authorized decision-maker to be found, for the decision-maker to be adequately informed and apprised of various alternatives, and actually to decide what to do.

A familiar difficulty with computer-launched weapons is that error may occur at the satellite or radar detection end of the system, or within the computer launch-decision equipment itself. The recent misinterpretation of a flight of geese over Vermont as an array of incoming Soviet missiles would have initiated a rapid countdown procedure leading finally to the "launch upon warning" of U.S. missiles toward the Soviet Union. The Soviet Union, accurately recognizing incoming U.S. missiles, would launch by computer their missile force. The result would be hundreds of millions of deaths, and no one would have made a decision.[3]

The Other Counterforce Weapons

Trident II:

The Trident II submarine-launched ballistic missile would presumably be ready for deployment by the end of the 1980s. It would be able to hit Soviet missile silos with a high degree of accuracy, and thus, with the MX, it can be viewed as a "first strike" weapon. The submarines carrying the Trident II would hold 24 such missiles, with each missile having 7 warheads. If it were to fire an average payload of 75 to 100 kilotons per warhead, a Trident II submarine could destroy 408 cities or military targets with a blast 5 times the force of the Hiroshima bomb. Trident expert Robert Aldridge writes: "A fleet of 30 Trident submarines would be able to deliver an unbelievable 12,240 nuclear warheads . . . 30 times

31

the number originally thought sufficient for strategic deterrence. Clearly, if Trident attains the accuracies the Navy seeks, it will constitute the ultimate first-strike weapon."[4]

Cruise:
Another of the new counterforce weapons is the Cruise missile. As an air-launched missile, the Cruise is a small, pilotless aircraft, 20 of which can be carried by a B-52 bomber. The Cruise is able to fly at extremely low altitudes, thus making radar detection very difficult. The missile is purported to be highly accurate and can put a 200-kiloton warhead directly on target. The sophisticated navigation system of the Cruise is based upon a terrain contour matching (TERCOM) sensor system that guides the missile by matching the terrain with a map of the target route stored in the computer.

An air-launched Cruise missile (ALCM) can be launched from as far away as 650 nautical miles from its target. This missile travels at sub-sonic speed. "Approaching hostile territory, it descends to within 100 feet of the surface to follow hills and valleys. Fifty miles from its target it drops to a mere fifty feet off the ground and then accelerates for its final dash."[5]

The sea-launched Cruise missile (SLCM) called "Tomahawk," is being designed for firing from a surface ship or a submarine. As with all Cruise missiles, this missile would present problems for arms limitation, however, since it can be hidden easily from observation. Therefore the question of compliance with treaty limitations is a major concern with regard to deploying this missile.

The ground-launched Cruise missile (GLCM) is being planned for deployment in Europe, as a replacement for tactical ballistic missiles. These Cruises would be fired from mobile launchers in Western Europe, and could strike all Soviet targets west of the Urals, thereby rendering vulnerable most of the Soviet industrial capacity and 40% of the Soviet population. The anticipated deployment of GLCMs and Pershing II intermediate range ballistic missiles is advocated by those who see a building-up of Warsaw Pact weapons targeted for Western Europe. Others, however, including the Center for Defense Information, believe that the combined nuclear capability of Britain, France, NATO aircraft and missile-carrying submarines already far exceeds the nuclear capability of the Warsaw Pact nations, and that deploying new weapons needlessly escalates the arms race in Europe.

A December 1979 NATO decision entails the substitution of 464 ground-launched Cruise missiles (GLCMs) beginning in 1983 and 108 Pershing II intermediate range ballistic missiles (IRBMs) by 1985 for certain existing U.S. weapons in Europe. Each weapon would be able to hit targets well inside the Soviet Union. The U.S. would retain control of the new weapons — a matter of increasing alarm to some Europeans. Thus, for example, Nobel laureate Anthony Ryle wrote from Great

Britain to *The New York Times* (October 7, 1980): "Many of us are unwilling to house on our soil nuclear weapons that are not under our government's control, on the principle of no annihilation without representation."

Nonetheless, as matters presently stand, the possibility of nuclear annihilation is real in Europe. In his *Department of Defense Annual Report, Fiscal Year 1982,* Harold Brown states, "Theater Nuclear Forces (TNF) visibly manifest the U.S. nuclear commitment to NATO and our willingness to use nuclear weapons in the defense of Europe if necessary."[6] No guarantee exists, of course, that a nuclear war in Europe —horrible in itself — would not escalate into the final apocalypse. And that Christians anywhere would in silence allow such unprecedented killing is unthinkable.

1. C.E.P. is a way of determining a missile's ability to land close to its target. It signifies the radius of a circle measured in nautical miles centered on the target within which half of the warheads fired at that target are expected to land.

2. Department of Defense, *Annual Report: Fiscal Year 1982.* Washington, D.C. January, 1981. p. 53.

3. Roger D. Speed, in *Strategic Deterrence in the 1980s.* (Stanford: Hoover Institution Press, 1979. pp. 72 & 74), and Richard Thaxton, in "Nuclear War by Computer Chip: How America Almost 'Launched on Warning'," *(The Progressive,* 1980), among others, point out the frightening dangers of launch upon warning strategies. Each writer urges the avoidance of such a policy.

4. Robert C. Aldridge, *The Counterforce Syndrome; A Guide to U.S. Nuclear and Strategic Doctrine.* Washington, D.C.: The Institute for Policy Studies, 1979. p. 35.

5. Aldridge, *ibid.,* p. 40.

6. Department of Defense, *ibid.,* p. 64.

DISCUSSION QUESTIONS
CHAPTER TWO:
NUCLEAR WEAPONS

1. How would you characterize the TRIAD defense capability of the United States?

2. How do you understand the corresponding defense capability of the Soviet Union?

3. Where do you think you are most secure: in the U.S. or in the Soviet Union?

4. Which side, do you think, has the stronger force?

5. Which side, do you think, is in the better position to take even the smallest step back from the next escalating step?

6. Is "deterrence" the same thing as, or different from, arms superiority? Why?

7. Does "limited nuclear war" seem likely? How would/could it remain limited?

8. If you were a Trident submarine commander, and you were reliably informed of a Soviet nuclear missile attack upon the U.S., would you fire your nuclear missiles at Soviet cities? Why or why not?

9. How would you feel about the U.S. firing nuclear missiles first at the Soviet Union, in an attempt to knock out Soviet missiles "pre-emptively"?

10. How would you feel about the U.S. responding to a first Soviet attack by firing at Soviet population centers?

11. Imagine that you are a Soviet policy-maker. You have learned that the U.S. is designing counterforce (high accuracy, high yield weapons). What would you recommend as a national security policy responding to this turn of events? Why?

3.
WHO ARE THE SOVIETS?

"O God, the Father of all, whose Son commanded us to love our enemies: Lead them and us from prejudice to truth; deliver them and us from hatred, cruelty, and revenge; and in your good time enable us all to stand reconciled before you; through Jesus Christ our Lord."
The Book of Common Prayer, p. 816.

The collect above reminds us that Jesus did not begin by asking us how we felt about our enemies; he simply commanded us to love them.

But who are my enemies? A certain man went down to Jericho and was beaten, robbed, and left for dead. A Samaritan, someone of a different cultural background, happened along and patched him up. Do you think the Samaritan was an enemy to that other or did he choose to be a neighbor?

Who tell us that others are our enemies? Why?

Is it possible that the real enemy is nuclear war?

Is there a Christian perspective on all humanity, or is there first and foremost a national perspective? If the former, an important spiritual discipline is to look upon the world from the vantage point of God — or the cross.

Jesus said, "pray for your enemies." We *can* pray for them, while we seek to understand them.

* * *

'I sing of arms and the man . . .' — Virgil's *Aeneid*

WHO ARE THE SOVIETS?

To provide an effective defense is one of the first obligations of government. To be overly trustful of the Soviet Union is to be naive; to be overly frightened of the Soviets is to be paranoid. Who are the Soviets, and what do they want? What basis in reality can be found to justify our hopes and fears concerning this nation in the nuclear age? If some clarity can be gained on these questions we might get a better sense of what is fitting for realistic security policies and programs. In the words of Alan Wolfe,

"If the Soviet Union really is a military threat to the American system, then it is impossible to object to taking any and all measures necessary to insure the preservation of the United States. But if the threat is not genuine — if it is exaggerated, distorted, and based upon self-serving needs — then the danger to America's democracy comes as much from within us as from without, for in such a case there would be pressure to expand the military budget, curtail basic freedoms, and restrict open access to government on the basis of a premise that was false."[1]

What salient aspects of Soviet life contribute to a Soviet perspective on the world?

The Soviet Experience of War

Knowledgeable observers of the people, culture, and government of the Soviet Union — such as former *New York Times* and *Washington Post* Moscow correspondents Hedrick Smith[2] and Robert G. Kaiser,[3] among others — have described the pervasive and persistent impact upon Soviet life of the World War II experience. Kaiser reports in 1975 that, "Thirty years after its conclusion the war remains a haunting presence in Soviet life — like a retarded child or a dying parent in the back room, a permanent piece of the emotional furniture."[4] And according to Hedrick Smith, "No Westerner visiting the Soviet Union can fail to be struck by the constant harping on the war, the everpresent theme of that holocaust . . . and the feeling that for Soviet people the war ended only yesterday."[5]

Smith describes the "monument of huge, stark tank traps" past which the visitor to Moscow travels from the airport. These are the reminders of how frighteningly close to Moscow the German armies came before they were driven back. The Odessa partisan hideouts, the Lithuanian statue of a gaunt mother, the Piskarevka Cemetery of Leningrad with its acres of graves, the Khatyn statue of a man tenderly holding his dying son, the memorials in the Northern Caucasus, the museum in Pskov — these and countless others are reminders of war to the Soviet people, and reminders more especially of the Russo-German war of 1940-1945. Military historian Theodore Ropp has called the Russo-German war "The greatest land war in history."[6]

In addition to devastated industries and cities, the Russians in World War II lost more people than in the terrible War of 1914-1918 and in their Civil War, combined. The Germans estimated 20 million Russian military and civilian dead, a tenth of the population. On their part, German losses were so high in Russia that an order to go to the Eastern front was viewed in the German army as the equivalent of a death sentence.

The point, withal, is that ample evidence exists that the meaning of war, its personal and social costs, is vivid in the minds of the Russian people. It seems most difficult to imagine that a people so devastated by war would wish to bring upon them the entire nuclear arsenal of the United States. It seems quite likely, too, that the Soviet people — knowing the meaning of war — know the meaning and value of peace.

Experiences Under Russian Leaders

Stalin

Without any question, the reign of Stalin, which lasted from 1929 to 1953, was a time of enormous suffering for the people of the Soviet Union. The notorious arrests, imprisonments, tortures, and deaths carried out by Stalin's political police victimized more people than did Hitler's holocaust. Though the exact numbers of deaths will never be known, it seems clear that several millions died in the forced collectivization of the peasants from 1929 to 1933, and in the general terror that followed until Stalin's death. The monstrous crimes perpetrated in the chain of labor camps known as the Gulag Archipelago, and in the terrors of other camps and mental hospitals, are sufficient to warrant the world's strongest moral condemnation.

The Stalin era also saw some genuine achievements, and these should be given their due. Soviet life changed from a mostly primitive agricultural economy to a primarily urban and industrial one. Widespread illiteracy was largely overcome. The Soviet Union had done more than any other nation to defeat the Hitler menace, and by the end of World War II had emerged as the dominant force in Eastern Europe and had become one of the major world powers.

Khrushchev

In 1956, however, a new climate began to characterize the life of the Soviet Union. At this time Nikita Khruschev's "de-Stalinization" effort commenced. It was an attempt to reverse the outrageous process of terrorism and to improve the psychological and cultural quality of life for the Soviet people. Khrushchev delivered a four-hour "secret speech" on the night of February 24, 1956, to a closed session of the twentieth Party Congress. In this he exposed many of the cruelties of the Stalin regime. Though Khrushchev even failed to mention a number of Stalin's abuses, he did succeed in setting a stage for a relatively more moderate political climate in Russia. By 1957 a new theme in Soviet literature had arisen, in which the horrors of the labor camps were described, though usually in a somewhat guarded fashion.

The plan to discredit Stalin and his terrorist methods was most dramatically apparent in Khrushchev's October 1961 speech to the twenty-second Party Congress. In contrast to the 1956 speech, this one was public. Comprehensive and detailed revelations of Stalinist crimes were presented to the Congress. Some of the crimes thus described had occurred with the complicity of officials still living.

During the following years, Stalin's military blunders of World War II (some of them of catastrophic magnitude) were reported to the Soviet people. The terrors of the camps were fully elaborated, perhaps most memorably by Solzhenitsyn's *One Day in the Life of Ivan Denisovich,* in 1962. The previously unmentioned forced collectivization of 125 million peasants from 1929 to 1933 was soon revealed in all its tragic magnitude: the overwhelming damage to Soviet agriculture and peasant life, the forced mass migrations, the famine, and the winter hardships in particular.

A reaction against "de-Stalinization" set in. This was manifested in the October 1964 ouster of Krushchev from Central Committee leadership, though other factors also bore upon Khrushchev's fate, including the failure of his agricultural policies and the Cuban missile embarrassment. Many thought that "de-Stalinization" had gone too far. Among those were persons who themselves had perpetrated some of the Stalinist abuses. Others included people who had endured enormous danger and hardship in Stalin's army and who could not accept what was now being said concerning his military ineptness and even cowardice. Still others — upper level bureaucrats — feared a general skepticism towards, and overall breakdown of, authoritarian government. And there were many common people who believed that at the least, the advances made during the Stalin years ought to be recognized and appreciated.

Brezhnev
By late 1965 a new leadership group began to exercise dominance in Soviet public life. This group, which included Leonid Brezhnev, recognized

the political value of polishing the Stalin image and consequently began to reverse the "de-Stalinization" process. With the February 1966 trial of two prominent anti-Stalin intellectuals, the consolidation of pro-Stalin reaction was effectively demonstrated. The chief consequence of this turn of events was the driving of several important Soviet intellectuals into dissident positions. Sakharov, the Medvedevs, and Solzhenitsyn were among the dissident group. The *samizdat* literature of protest was born at this time, but despite its aim, the Brezhnev reaction to Khrushchev's reforms was effectively accomplished. Certainly the end of Khrushchev was viewed with justifiable alarm by the United States. A period of about four years was required for Brezhnev to feel secure enough to negotiate with the West. Eventually, Brezhnev's 1971 stance, called the "peace program," helped to create detente, and its first priority was to seek to control the increase in strategic nuclear weapons.

Domestic Problems

As for the Soviet Union today, the Smithsonian's *Wilson Quarterly* recently chronicled a number of significant internal problems. Chief among these are a very low (2%) annual economic growth rate, a growing shortage of skilled labor, inefficient agricultural production, an enormous military budget, limited technological progress, uncertain energy availability, and rising death rates coupled with falling birth rates.

To get a sense of internal Soviet problems, it seems useful to look at one problem, labor supply, in depth as an example. The coming dip in the Soviet labor supply will not easily be offset by increased productivity because of a predicted steady decrease in Soviet capital formation. Moreover, there is the factor of ethnic diversity to complicate things. Murray Feshbach, Chief of the U.S. Census Bureau's U.S.S.R. Population, Employment, and Research and Development branch, notes that "The U.S.S.R.'s ethnic groups range from Eskimo to German. In 1977, more than 40 languages of instruction were used in Soviet schools; in 1979 the Soviet census counted 22 'nationalities' with populations of more than a million."[9]

The legacy of the Stalin purges, and the 15 million males alone lost during the Second World War, figure significantly in the present Soviet predicament. But more recently there has been a remarkable increase in the 20 to 44-year-old mortality rate, with a corresponding reduction in male life expectancy from 66 to 63 years. The major cause of this demographic change is alcoholism. Another cause of the projected shortage of labor is the "single sex cities," in which men are concentrated in cities of heavy industry, with women in cities of textile and other light industrial manufacturing. Rising infant mortality rates are due to poor pre-natal and post-natal care, a high abortion rate, and fetal alcohol syndrome.

A significant exception to this overall pattern is the Soviet Central Asian (Turkic) population group which is growing markedly. These 40 million Asian Muslims, in contrast to the Russian and other Slavic groups of the U.S.S.R., were relatively untouched by the Stalin terror and World War II, and are generally opposed to alcohol consumption and abortion. They will have grown by 50% to 60 million by the century's end. The implication for Soviet planners of this population shift appears ominous, because relationships between the Muslim groups and the ethnic Russians have been consistently troubled. The European Russians have controlled power politically and militarily in Muslim areas since the Red Army victories of 1920 and 1921. As the entire Soviet nation is forced to rely increasingly upon its Muslim population for industrial and military personnel, historical ethnic conflicts will unquestionably become a serious factor in the overall Soviet situation. Brezhnev and his successors will have major internal challenges concerning military and industrial preparedness, as well as formidable external challenges from the United States and elsewhere. The diversion of time, energy, and resources to the arms race with the United States means that a swift and effective approach to solving serious internal problems (difficult to solve under the best of conditions) is impossible.

Arms and Technology

The highest economic priority of the Soviet Union is support of the arms industry. All civilian skills, materials, energy, and other resources are diverted as needed to the military sector in the amounts and kinds deemed necessary by Soviet planners. Moreover, the highest standards of quality control are exercised in the military area. The costs to the Soviets of their military production are enormous, though probably unknown even to the Russians themselves. What is very clear is that despite overall economic sluggishness and comparative technological lag, the Soviets are willing to do whatever is necessary at least to keep pace with the United States in the matter of arms.[10] Consequently, U.S. arms strategies based upon achieving clear-cut and lasting superiority over the Russians seem blind to Soviet persistence and determination as demonstrated over the last 35 years.

Here it is instructive to summarize the post-World War II history of Soviet scientific and technological research as it has had significance for U.S. policy decisions and hence for the continuing arms race.

Daniel Yergin[11] recounts the flight of a U.S. bomber over the North Pacific Ocean on September 3, 1949. At 18,000 feet the atmospheric radioactivity level recorded by that B-29 seemed elevated, and yet not much was made of the report. During the days that followed, however, increased radioactivity was noticed in the winds that drifted over North America and then into Europe. Soviet radio, TASS, confirmed on September 25, 1949 that the U.S.S.R. had indeed exploded an atomic device. Although not yet able to deliver such weapons by the means available to the United States, the Soviets nevertheless had become the second nation to possess the atomic bomb.

By August 1953, four years later, the Soviets tested a thermonuclear weapon, matching the United States in this capability. On October 4, 1957, Sputnik I was launched as the first satellite, and four years after that Yuri Gagarin became the first human in space. Soviet technology was not sufficiently advanced to enable the firing of missiles from submarines until the mid-1960s, and Soviet Intercontinental Ballistic Missiles comparable to those of the United States were not deployed until the late 1960s.

The United States and other nations incorrectly interpreted Soviet successes in the 1950s and early 1960s, especially the first Sputnik launch, as signs of highly sophisticated military technology in the Soviet Union. The U.S. determination to beat the Russians to the moon in retrospect seems to have been a sure bet since the Soviets (in Robert G. Kaiser's words) "never had the capacity to fly to the moon or even to conduct very extensive experiments outside the earth's atmosphere."[12]

In contrast to the Soviets the U.S. space efforts of the 1960s consisted in impressive technological advances. Soviet rocketry has made only limited progress; even today the Soviets appear to possess no dependable solid-fuel rocket, as noted earlier. The July 1975 link-up between U.S. and Soviet spaceships was accomplished on the Russian side by a rocket not radically different from the World War II V-2 developed by the Germans. As Robert Kaiser notes, "The Russians have never mastered high energy rocket fuels, and still use kerosene."[13]

The 1957 Sputnik launch, which startled the world, had occurred mainly because the Soviets were practical enough to clump together four large engines at the base of a single rocket. The technology was not especially innovative. The Sputnik itself was only a small sphere containing a radio beeper.

The technology that thrust the first human into space entailed the combining of five clusters of four rockets each. Technologically this strategy did not show imaginative genius, though it did represent a certain practicality. The advanced metallurgical technology which marks the power and reliability of U.S. rocket engines has eluded the Soviets to this day.

Certainly the scientific and technological capability of the Soviet Union ought not to be minimized. The Russian ability and willingness especially to mobilize resources to achieve specific objectives is most impressive. Unmistakably clear is that though the United States possesses technological superiority over the Soviets, the Russians are determined to keep pace; only for them it takes a little longer. Despite frequent bureaucratic and political impediments, the Soviets seem able to make the most of what they have in the area of military technology. Yet something important also is conveyed by the fact that of all the Nobel prizes for science awarded since 1920, well over 100 have gone to U.S. scientists, about 50 to British scientists and fewer than 10 to Soviet scientists. These figures tend to show that at least some estimates of Soviet research wizardry may be unduly flattering.

Soviet Intentions

What are Soviet intentions concerning the U.S.? And what, more exactly, are Soviet intentions regarding the nuclear arms race? It is impossible to develop clear answers to these questions, since in foreign affairs *stated* intentions may not necessarily be taken as sincerely motivated, and since intentions change in response to changing world conditions. Yet it is not unreasonable to assume that in such areas as world regard, self-respect, a strengthened overall economy, smooth internal functioning, peace, order, and the like, the Soviets have desires similar to those of the U.S. Such a general inference might be drawn according to common sense.

Some other influences of Soviet intentions might be made more specifically, though more tentatively, from the peculiarity of Soviet history. The considerable costs of World War II would seem to make the possibility of war both more urgent and more fearsome to the Soviets than to others whose homelands were not so devastated as Soviet homelands or not devastated at all. A second inference to be drawn is that because of all its aforementioned internal problems, the Soviet Union seems likely to desire the fullest possible commitment of its total resources to internal matters. The poor economy, labor problems, rampant alcoholism, poor health care, inferior civilian industrial products, and other problems, mean that continued massive military expenditures are costly to civilians who must remain patient with a troubled civilian economy. A third inference to be drawn concerning Soviet intentions is that since the Soviets have consistently kept pace with U.S. military technology, though it takes them some time to do it, they will continue to do so. The historical records shows unambiguously that U.S. weapons "superiority" has never been conceded by the Soviets. There is no reason at all to doubt that the Soviets intend to be equal with the

United States in the military area. Indeed, for the U.S. to ignore this obvious fact only postpones the day when sincere U.S. negotiation attempts may begin as a means to de-escalate the frightening nuclear arms race.

Another historical basis upon which a reasonable inference might be made concerning Soviet arms intentions is the record of arms limitation talks. Numerous arms control conferences have been convened since the Second World War. In 1946, for example, the U.N. General Assembly's first resolution called for the elimination of all atomic weapons and any other weapons of comparable effect. President Eisenhower's December 8, 1953 address to the United Nations proposed that the nuclear superpowers "begin to diminish the potential destructive power of the world's atomic stockpiles." Eight years later, in addressing the same body, President Kennedy stated that "mankind must put an end to war — or war will put an end to mankind." He added, "The risks inherent in disarmament pale in comparison to the risks inherent in an unlimited arms race." An important step forward was made as the U.S. and the U.S.S.R. in 1963 agreed to stop testing nuclear weapons in any environment where fallout would occur outside the country testing the weapon. Each country has abided by this agreement. But the Nuclear Non-Proliferation Treaty of 1968 has not had clear success. The Anti-ballistic Missile Treaty of 1972 between the U.S. and the Soviet Union, signed as part of SALT I, does contain an agreement by both powers to avoid building defensive missile systems against incoming nuclear missiles. Both sides honored this agreement.

The 1972 SALT I agreement, however, has been unsuccessful in controlling the growth of strategic offensive weapons. Tactical nuclear weapons (the kind that are deployed in Europe) and conventional weapons were never subject to the SALT provisions and hence have not been limitable by this treaty even in principle. Generally speaking, SALT I limited the numbers of deployable nuclear weapons, but not the kinds and amounts of new strategic weapons. Paradoxically, by limiting the numbers of vehicles for delivering nuclear warheads, SALT I tacitly encouraged the development of multiple warheads that could be carried by each vehicle. Hence the emergence of MIRV'd warheads (3 to 10 to a missile) for Intercontinental and Submarine Launched Ballistic Missiles. SALT I also contributed in its paradoxical way to increasing the sophistication, accuracy, and therefore destructive capability of submarine and bomber forces on each side. Clearly the first SALT agreement did not accomplish what the most hopeful diplomats on each side desired, but it did open a door wider to the continuing process of negotiation.

The outrageous 1979 Soviet invasion of Afghanistan caused President Carter to withdraw from the U.S. Senate the initialled SALT II agreement, which was to last until 1985. The SALT II treaty essentially recapitulates the 1974 Vladivostok Accord, which puts some quantitative limits upon the number of offensive strategic weapons launchers deployed by each side, qualitatively limits the weapons themselves, and provides means to check compliance by each side. Critics of SALT II assert that the treaty would only legitimize the nuclear arms race since it does not aim at a reduction of nuclear arms. Advocates of SALT II, however, point to the necessity of at least maintaining a negotiating climate of mutual understanding. They recognize the need to improve SALT II and to keep the negotiating process alive. President Reagan is on record as desiring real arms reductions, rather than simply putting ceilings on arms deployment. The discouraging history of past arms control attempts does not diminish, of course, the hope that Mr. Reagan and the Soviets will make significant progress in the future. For their part, the Soviets did participate in the SALT II talks and they have repeatedly expressed their desire for a resumption of arms limitation conferences. One does not have to approve the Afghanistan debacle in order to accept Soviet sincerity in wanting to control nuclear arms. In the face of mounting risks of nuclear war, the sincerity of Soviet intentions seems worth assuming.

U.S. Perceptions of the Soviet Threat

While the remote origins of U.S.-Soviet hostility might be found in the enormous crimes of the early Stalin era, the visible sign to the Soviets of U.S. skepticism was the withholding of official recognition of the Soviet government from its beginning until 1933. The pragmatic basis for military cooperation between the U.S. and U.S.S.R. during the Second World War tended to draw the two countries together, as the United States delivered considerable amounts of support to the U.S.S.R. under the Lend-Lease arrangement.

The positive atmosphere of cooperation at Yalta, near the war's end, lasted only as long as Roosevelt lived (he died within two months) and Churchill remained prime minister of Great Britain (he was replaced by Attlee within five months). The common goal of defeating Hitler, which had been the basis of the Grand Alliance, soon existed no longer. Could a more positive foundation for cooperation be found? On September 14, 1945 Stalin told U.S. Senator Claude Pepper at the Kremlin, "We shall have to find a new basis for our close relations in the future, and that will not be easy." Then Stalin, the former Russian Orthodox seminarian continued, "Christ said, 'Seek and ye shall find.' "[14] But the glue of the Grand Alliance did not hold. World War II's end found the United States with an atomic weapons monopoly and a growing distrust of the U.S.S.R. This skepticism was to take two forms, differing only in the degree to which military force was to be used or threatened by the United States in U.S.-Soviet relations.

Daniel Yergin, of Harvard's Center for International Affairs, offers two terms as useful for symbolizing the two basic U.S. views of the Soviet threat. The first he describes as the "Riga Axioms," consisting of an emphasis upon Russia as a dangerous enemy. (Riga is the Latvian city from which U.S. study of the Soviet Union was undertaken during the 1917-1940 era. Grave interpretations of Soviet behaviour were made in Riga and sent to Washington from that observation post.) The Yergin expression means that various individuals and groups in the United States can be called "Riga" in their views when those views see the Soviets as essentially expansionist and as requiring firm and perhaps forcible resolve from the U.S.

The other symbol, which places emphasis upon diplomacy rather than upon the immediate threat of force, is the "Yalta Axioms." (Yalta, of course, is the city in which the United States, the United Kingdom, and the Soviet Union agreed to work jointly in the post-1945 world.) "Yalta" and "Riga" have in common a regard for the Soviet Union as an adversary, but the Yalta Axioms also regard co-existence with the Soviets as possible without ready reliance upon military force. In the next chapter we shall examine a current instance of each view, to see which might be more fitting to a realistic view of the world and to our Christian self-understanding.

1. Alan Wolfe, *The Rise and Fall of the "Soviet Threat": Domestic Sources of the Cold War Consensus.* Washington: Institute for Policy Studies. 1979. (94 pp.) p. 2. Used by permission.

2. Hedrick Smith, *The Russians.* New York: ©1976. Hedrick Smith. (706 pp.) Reprinted by permission of TIMES BOOKS, a division of Quadrangle/The New York Times Book Co., Inc.

3. Robert G. Kaiser, *Russia: The People and The Power.* ©1976 by Robert G. Kaiser (New York: Atheneum. 1976.) Used by permission of Atheneum Publishers.

4. Kaiser, p. 275 (paperback edition). See above.

5. Smith, p. 420.

6. Theodore Ropp, *War in the Modern World.* Dunham: Duke University Press. 1959. (400 pp.) p. 324.

7. Andrei D. Sakharov, *Progress, Coexistence and Intellectual Freedom,* with Introduction, Afterword and Notes by Harrison E. Salisbury. New York: W. W. Norton & Co. 1968. (158 pp.) p. 12. Used by permission.

8. Sakharov, *Ibid.,* p. 27.

9. Murray Feshback, "A Different Crisis," *The Wilson Quarterly.* Winter, 1981. (pp. 117-125) p. 123.

10. Kaiser, p. 383. See above.

11. Daniel Yergin, *Shattered Peace: The Origins of The Cold War and the National Security State.* Boston: Houghton Mifflin Co. 1978. (526 pp.)

12. Kaiser, p. 321. See above.

13. *Ibid.*

14. Box 46, Pepper papers, quoted in Yergin, p. 4.

DISCUSSION QUESTIONS
CHAPTER THREE:
WHO ARE THE SOVIETS?

1. How would you characterize the people of the Soviet Union? How would you characterize the Soviet government?

2. How would you assess the Soviet consciousness of war and its costs?

3. Do you think the Soviet leadership desires war with the United States? Why?

4. Do you think the Soviet leadership fears the U.S.? Why?

5. What can be said with confidence concerning Soviet intentions?

6. Does our Christian faith apply to the question of taking risks for arms control *versus* risking a continuing arms escalation? If yes, why?

7. Is it possible to apply Christian spirituality to the problems of living peaceably with the Soviets? If yes, how might this be done?

4.

U.S. SECURITY STRATEGIES

"O God, you made us in your own image and redeemed us through Jesus your Son: look with compassion on the whole human family; take away the arrogance and hatred which infect our hearts; break down the walls that separate us; unite us in bonds of love; and work through our struggle and confusion to accomplish your purposes on earth; that, in your good time, all nations and races may serve you in harmony around your heavenly throne; through Jesus Christ our Lord."

The Book of Common Prayer, p. 815

The prayer for the Human Family describes with equal force the woeful reality of our human condition, and the Christian vision of a unified humanity, all nations and races.

The compassion of Christ benefits our paradoxical condition: made in God's image — but arrogant and hate-filled; redeemed — but divided and confused. Yet we struggle to accomplish the divine purposes on earth: if in harmony around the heavenly throne, then in harmony here and now. Thus our course as Christians is charted, our hope is warranted, our values and commitments sustained, by a worldly vision and a heavenly promise.

Our vision of the world and of its people is conditioned not only by what we see, but what we imagine and look for. We believe what we see, but we see what we believe.

We have evidence that this one, or this other, is our enemy or our neighbor. In the spiritual life of the soul we are predisposed more in one direction or the other. Some see the glass half-filled; others see it half-empty.

This Russian factory worker goes to work as I do. She eats lunch and later comes home, as I do. In the evening she reads or spends time with her family, as I do. She hates herself sometimes, as I do; at other times she is kind to herself and gives of herself to others, as I do.

She is my enemy? She is my sister? We are separated by walls? We are united because Christ loves us both?

How I look upon this other — this worker, this political leader, this soldier, this Russian, this American — expresses and determines, in the deepest spiritual sense, who I am.

How shall we look upon the Russians?

*   *   *

SALT II

U.S. SECURITY STRATEGIES

Daniel Yergin's alternative ways of viewing the Soviet Union are by the Riga Axioms, stressing a ready military response to the Soviets, and the Yalta Axioms, stressing more a negotiating response. We shall examine a leading instance of each point of view in the present chapter.

A Riga Point of View: Norman Podhoretz

The Riga point of view is expressed eloquently by the Committee on the Present Danger, one of whose able members is Norman Podhoretz. Mr. Podhoretz presents his case in *The Present Danger.*[1] This book begins with the assertion that the seizure of U.S. hostages in Iran marks the end of one period of U.S. history, while the Soviet invasion of Afghanistan begins another, and the assertion that the significant polarity of world relations has not changed to "North-South," but remains "East-West." Mr. Podhoretz also believes that a subtle but real shift in power has recently occurred, to the relative advantage of the Soviet Union and the disadvantage of the United States.

Norman Podhoretz cites the March 1947 Truman Doctrine as the beginning of the "containment" policy of the United States against "Soviet imperialism," and he believes that this policy (of which he approves) lasted until the Nixon detente program of 1969. The Truman Doctrine laid down that "it must be the policy of the United States to support free people who are resisting attempted subjugation by armed minorities or by outside pressure."[2]

Mr. Podhoretz understands George Kennan's "Mr. X" article in the July 1947 *Foreign Affairs* to have stressed a military as well as a political strategy to contain the Soviets. Though the Kennan theory of containment was subsequently repudiated by its author (Podhoretz tells us), it warranted the formation of NATO and, "in principle," the U.S. intervention in Korea and Vietnam.

President Kennedy's decision to send U.S. "advisers" to Vietnam was justified by the policy of containment. The major questions concerning such a decision were of a tactical sort; i.e., questions of whether U.S. involvement could be effective militarily in that unique context. Only as the war dragged on were more fundamental questions raised concerning the reasons for U.S. involvement. This brought things to a turning point. The insufficiency and variation of answers to such questions led to a public skepticism concerning "containment" policy, confidence in U.S. power, and the moral credibility of the U.S. as a force for good in world affairs generally. A "new national mood of self-doubt and self-disgust" eroded the "domestic base on which containment had rested."[3]

The Truman Doctrine was replaced by the Nixon Doctrine of "strategic retreat," to use Podhoretz's words, or "detente," in official language. The immediate focus of the Nixon policy was the gradual withdrawal of U.S. forces from the increasingly unpopular Vietnam War and the gradual equipping of Vietnamese replacement forces. More abstractly, the Nixon-Kissinger theory called for the limitation of U.S. power worldwide by supplying military aid to local, indigenous forces. The subsequent failure of this approach in Vietnam was coupled with the involvement of Cubans in Angola and takeovers by pro-Soviet governments in Laos, Ethiopia, Mozambique, Afghanistan, and Cambodia. Mr. Podhoretz believes that these events should arouse alarm in the United States. He does not state why.

The Podhoretz view is that, not wanting to be embarrassed by another Cuban missile crisis, the Soviets embarked upon, ". . . the greatest military build-up in the peacetime history of the world." At the time, the U.S. was, ". . . standing still and even slipping back" in the arms race.[4] As a result, the world balance of power would likely shift in favor of the Soviet Union. Podhoretz, however, seems unwilling to consider the possible effect upon Soviet feelings of insecurity of President Kennedy's "eyeball to eyeball" challenge.

Later the collapse of the Carter "mature restraint" policy came with the seizing of the U.S. embassy in Teheran and the Soviet incursion into Afghanistan. The presumed vulnerability of Persian Gulf oil to Soviet seizure gave rise to the new Carter doctrine that "An attempt by any outside force to gain control of the Persian Gulf region will be regarded as an assault on the vital interests of the United States." Such an adventure "will be repelled by any means necessary, including military force."[5] This doctrine marked a departure from detente and a return to containment. There is what Podhoretz sees as a "window of opportunity," symbolizing the Soviet opportunity to seize oil fields and "dominate the West" while U.S. "resolve" is minimal or altogether absent. The process currently underway, Mr. Podhoretz believes, leads finally to the "Finlandization of America," which is to him a "new species of surrender . . . a gradual but steady process of accommodation to Soviet wishes and demands."[6] But one might question whether the historical parallels between Soviet designs upon Finland, which were heroically and effectively repelled 40 years ago, and the situation between the Soviets and the U.S. today, are apt. Podhoretz does not help us see how "Finlandization" applies to us today.

Norman Podhoretz is alarmed about the "Vietnamization" of the past, present and future, as in his view "pacifist ideologues" have influenced a climate in the U.S. of "undifferentiated fear, loathing, and revulsion" concerning war. Thus the United States itself is now "foremost among the things not worth dying for." The legacy of anti-Vietnam-War sentiment is present in "Anti-Americanism today." Instances of "Anti-Americanism" views are found, for example, in the still current idea that the main obstacle to nuclear disarmament is the American military establishment and that unilateral reductions by the United States are all that is needed to make the Soviets follow suit. They are present in the idea that Americans consume more than their "fair share" of resources and that a voluntary reduction in the American standard of living (a kind of unilateral economic disarmament) is all that is needed to facilitate a more equitable distribution of wealth around the world. And they are present in the notion that the United States is the guilty party in every situation that arises. It is our fault that the Khmer Rouge murdered nearly half the population of Cambodia (because we drove them to desperate measures); it is our fault that the hostages were taken in Iran (because we supported the Shah for so many years); it is even our fault that the Soviets invaded Afghanistan (because by questioning the SALT treaty and taking steps to strengthen our defenses, we simultaneously frightened them and removed their incentive to restraint).[7] Mr. Podhoretz does not specifically identify those who presumably make such statements, nor does he show an openness for the possibility of some slight truth in the views he characterizes in such stark terms.

Against the "soporific forces" of appeasement that lead to "Finlandization" stands the hope of "the new nationalism." In part the new nationalism has been articulated by, ". . . a group of intellectuals often labelled 'neo-conservative' but who might more accurately have been described as 'neo-nationalists.' " These intellectuals, who include Mr. Podhoretz himself, hold a, ". . . highly positive view of the values implicit in the constitutional and institutional structure of American civilization" and a ". . . belief that the survival of liberty and democracy requires a forceful American presence in the world." The neo-nationalist intellectuals were influential partly because "they were able to best their opponents in argument," and partly because people recognized the horrors inflicted by Communists upon Indochinese people, which made ". . . the idea that the American role in Vietnam had been immoral or criminal . . . harder and harder to maintain . . ." Moreover, the continued attempts by the Soviet Union to attain nuclear superiority undermined the notion that the U.S. "was the cause of the nuclear arms race." Currently the new nationalism is locked in a "literally fateful struggle" with the culture of appeasement in the United States.[8]

The essential ingredient to proper thinking about our present danger is our recognition that the Soviet Union is unlike any other nation. It is a revolutionary state, exactly as Hitler's Germany was, ". . . in the sense that it wishes to create a new international order in which it would be the dominant power and whose character would be determined by its national wishes and its ideological dictates."[9] The freedoms and the prosperity currently found in the U.S. would disappear in the new Soviet order. The Russians are destructive of political structures and economies: "The only thing the Soviets seem good at is producing nuclear bombs and missiles."[10]

Are we willing to resist the Soviets?, asks Podhoretz. Could the Chinese effectively resist? (To this Podhoretz says No.) Would the NATO allies resist? (Not likely, unless the U.S. leads with resolute strength.) What about defending a "free world" by supporting right-wing dictators? Podhoretz: "Yet the United States was leading a free-world alliance in the entirely meaningful sense that every free society in the world was either a member of the alliance or under its protection. It is true that out of prudential considerations, like the need for bases, certain authoritarian regimes and right-wing dictatorships were also included in the alliance. But in view of the fact that such associations were important in holding back the single greatest and most powerful threat to freedom on the face of the earth, they could be justified as an unfortunate political and military necessity."[11]

To support "certain authoritarian regimes and right-wing dictatorships" seems justifiable if one decides to believe, as Podhoretz believes, that the world is a battleground between the forces of light (led by the U.S.) and the forces of dark (the Soviet Union). Christians are usually not so political in their religion. Is it not rather more true that there is a little light and dark everywhere, and that at the least it is difficult to support right-wing cruelty simply because it claims to oppose left-wing cruelty?

Podhoretz ends his book by quoting George Kennan's 1947 *Foreign Affairs* article which at that time called upon the people of the United States to accept "the responsibilities of moral and political leadership that history plainly intended them to bear."[12] In face of the "Finlandization" which he fears is before us, the Kennan exhortation of 1947 appears to Podhoretz to be all the more compelling today.

A Yalta Point of View: George Kennan

It should be noted, certainly, that the George Kennan of 1947 is not the Kennan of 1981. On May 19, 1981 Kennan told a Washington audience who honored him with the Einstein Peace Prize that, ". . . adequate words are lacking to express the full seriousness of our present situation," which is that both the U.S. and Soviet policies are ultimately sanctioned by ". . . a type and volume of weaponry that could not possibly be used without utter disaster for everyone concerned."[13]

Kennan notes that grave warnings concerning the futility of nuclear war have come from a vast array of eminent persons. Yet today we and the Soviets have fashioned such quantities of horrendously destructive nuclear weapons at, ". . . levels of redundancy of such grotesque dimensions as to defy national understanding." Kennan continues, the nuclear bomb is "the most useless weapon ever invented." This weapon, ". . . is only something with which, in a moment of petulance or panic, you perpetrate upon the helpless people of another country such fearful acts of destruction as no sane person would ever wish to have upon his conscience."

Certainly, deterrence is important, but "well less than 20 per cent" of the current U.S. nuclear arsenal could easily dissuade the most criminal plans of any adversary to attack the U.S. How did we get into "this dangerous mess?" Kennan chronicles the history of escalations, placing the greater responsibility for escalation upon the U.S. and its persistent weapons technology advances. The way out of our predicament is surely not by means of "victory," which is nothing short of a "plain and unalterable catastrophe."

The first step in finding a way out is to recognize that nuclear weapons, as weapons of mass and indiscriminant destruction, are qualitatively different from all other weapons: "Whoever does not understand that when it comes to nuclear weapons the whole concept of relative advantage is illusory — whoever does not understand that when you are talking about preposterous quantities of overkill the relative sizes of arsenals have no serious meaning — whoever does not understand that the danger lies not in the possibility that someone else might have more missiles and warheads than you do, but in the very existence of these unconscionable quantities of highly poisonous explosives, and their existence, above all, in hands as weak and shaky and undependable as those of ourselves or our adversaries or any other mere human beings: whoever does not understand these things is never going to guide us out of this increasingly dark and menacing forest of bewilderments into which we have all wandered."[14]

Kennan's proposal is that a bold new action should be taken, one that is justified in its freshness by the urgency of our predicament. Kennan holds that President Reagan, after proper consultation with Congress, should ". . . propose to the Soviet government an immediate across-the-boards reduction by 50 percent of the nuclear arsenals" of both nations. This reduction would affect, ". . . in equal measure all forms of the weapons, strategic, medium-range, and tactical, as well as all means of their delivery." Kennan addresses issues of the methods for verifying compliance and safely disposing of the dismantled weapons parts.

Concerning risks, Kennan concludes: "Is it possible to conceive of any dangers greater than those that lie at the end of the collision course on which we are now embarked? And if not, why choose the greater — why choose, in fact, the greatest — of all risks, in the hopes of avoiding the lesser ones?

"We are confronted here with two courses. At the end of one lies hope — faint hope, if you will —uncertain hope, hope surrounded with dangers, if you insist — but hope nevertheless. At the end of the other lies, so far as I am able to see, no hope at all. Can there be — in the light of our duty not just to ourselves (for we are all going to die sooner or later) but of our duty to our own kind, our duty to the continuity of the generations, our duty to the great experiment of civilized life on this rare and rich and marvelous planet — can there really be, in the light of these claims on our loyalty, any question as to which course we should adopt?"[15]

The Domestic Sources of U.S. Hostility to the Soviets

Why does "hard line" U.S. anti-Soviet sentiment prevail at certain times in our country? In his *Rise and Fall of the "Soviet Threat": Domestic Sources of the Cold War Consensus,*[16] Alan Wolfe develops his view that, ". . . in the past, U.S. perceptions of hostile Soviet intentions have increased, not when the Russians have become more aggressive or militaristic, but when certain constellations of political forces have come together within the United States to force the question of the Soviet Threat upon the American political agenda."[17] Wolfe finds ". . . no clear evidence either that the Russians are increasing their military strength relative to the United States or that the United States is falling behind the Soviets in armaments or 'resolve.' " Hence he thinks it impossible to provide a rational case for a strong military response to the Soviet Union, based upon the "Soviet Threat" itself.

Wolfe believes that 1980s analogies to the Nazi arms build-up of the 1930s are inaccurate, that U.S. and Soviet comparisons of military spending are simplistic and misleading, that indigenous Third World revolutions have indeed recently increased "but Soviet intervention has not," and that in fact the Soviet Union and the United States have worked together effectively in spite of official rhetoric to the contrary. Thus: "The U.S. tacitly acknowledged Soviet control over Eastern Europe in the 1940s, did not support the Hungarian revolt in the 1950s, and accepted the Soviet's drive for nuclear parity in the 1960s and 1970s. Likewise the Russians, over and above their anti-capitalist ideology, declined to sign a separate peace treaty with East Germany, backed down over Cuba, and agreed not to challenge directly the U.S. bombing of their allies in

Southeast Asia. In acts, if not always in speech, each superpower has recognized that it shares an interest with the other in preserving a world order from would-be challengers.

"This search for accommodation between the two superpowers means that often they act in a less hostile manner than their rhetoric suggests. In recent years, for example, the Russians have bent over backwards to obtain a SALT treaty, refusing to break off negotiations when the Americans changed the terms of the discussion early in the Carter Administration. They agreed to Mutual and Balanced Force Reduction (MBFR) talks in Vienna at a time when the U.S. was considering unilateral troop withdrawals, hardly evidence of a desire to split the Atlantic Alliance or to overrun Western Europe. In the last Geneva talks about the Middle East before Camp David they were quite accommodating. They sought to preserve detente even while the U.S. broke all international rules of proper conduct in its bombing of Cambodia. If the extreme anti-Soviet views are correct, it becomes difficult to understand Russian eagerness for wheat deals, most favored nation trading status, cooperation in space, and other evidence of mutual support between the countries."[18]

Wolfe finds it curious that even though there may be contrasting views of Soviet intentions, frequently the more alarmist view prevails in the United States. He analyzes this phenomenon and concludes that it occurs because of five "common features" present in peak periods of anti-Soviet hostility. These five features are, 1) an imbalance in partisan politics, 2) major internal threats to the institution of the Presidency, 3) unusually severe interservice rivalry, 4) strong conflicts concerning the direction of U.S. foreign policy, and, 5) the emergence of strong political forces desiring greater federal spending to stimulate economic growth. After evaluating each factor in its post-World War II history, Alan Wolfe concludes that "The new cold war militancy" has ". . . more to do with the domestic politics of the late 1970s than . . . with the Soviet military build-up, or indeed with international politics at all."[19]

Using defense budget variations and the frequency of U.S. displays of military force as criteria, Mr. Wolfe identifies three historical "peaks" and two "valleys" in U.S. cold war hostility to the Soviets. The highlights of Wolfe's work are given here.

The Beginning of the Cold War
The 1948-1952 period in U.S. history was characterized by the formation of a view of the Soviet union as "globally aggressive" — when "equally plausible interpretations" of Soviet behavior could have construed that behavior in terms of "limited self-interest." A major factor in

the climate gathering at this time was the George Kennan "long telegram," sent from Moscow in February, 1946, which warned of Russian aggression. Kennan's influential article, "The Sources of Soviet Conduct," appeared in the July, 1947 *Foreign Affairs,* and this spoke ominously of the Soviet menace.

In March and April, 1948, the North Atlantic Treaty Organization (NATO) was created, which enabled the establishment of military bases close to the Russians, and in some instances established bases in countries bordering the Soviet Union. In June, 1948 the Berlin Blockade was initiated by the Soviets. This was countered by the highly successful Berlin Airlift, whose result was a costly political defeat for Stalin. (Robert G. Kaiser believes that the Berlin Blockade was, ". . . a fast, desperate effort to dissuade Britain, France, and America from establishing a West German state that could rearm and eventually threaten Russia again. Stalin felt helpless when the Americans challenged the blockade, and helpless again when they permitted the formation of a West German government."[20]

The April, 1950 National Security Council position paper, NSC-68, proposed the commitment of economic resources consistent with the earlier Kennan theories regarding Soviet expansionism. This document called for a tripling of the military budget and proved important in the creation of a strong anti-Soviet climate at the highest government level. At the heart of NSC-68 were two curious gaps in logic, one being the analogy of the Soviet Union to Nazi Germany, and the other being an explanation of why internal authoritarianism is causally linked to an alleged external expansionism.

Alan Wolfe characterizes the 1952-1957 "valley" in anti-Soviet hostility as the "overwhelming desire for normalcy" in the United States. The stiff rhetoric of John Foster Dulles against the Soviet Union was counterbalanced by Republican fiscal restraint. As a result, actual military spending and military shows of force during this time were minimal. The Riga view of the Soviets as contained in NSC-68 was not effectual in the world of practical affairs.

A new document became the focus of another peak of anti-Soviet hostility. This was the report of a study commission chaired by Rowan Gaither; hence the document, entitled *Deterrence and Survival in the Nuclear Age,* came to be known more simply as "the Gaither Report." The heart of this document consisted of a chart showing past U.S. military supremacy over the Soviets, present (1957) equality with the Soviets, and future military vulnerability to the Soviets. Wolfe writes, "In the strongest possible terms, the Report urged an immediate turn to high defense budgets and an effort to indoctrinate the public into a crisis mentality."[21]

Democratic party contenders for President in 1960 employed a strategy of faulting the incumbent administration for not keeping national security at an optimal level. John Kennedy increased the military budget by 15% in his first year as president, tripled draft calls, and advocated an expanded program of civil defense. Most dangerously, Kennedy ". . . let it be known that he would welcome a head-to-head confrontation with the Soviet Union, something Eisenhower had tried to avoid."[22] President Kennedy's Secretary of State, Dean Rusk, promulgated the domino theory of Soviet aggression. Like Maxwell Taylor's *Uncertain Trumpet,* this theory accomplished the dubious task of setting a Cold War context for any outbreak of local hostilities. The possibility that a local outburst might have nothing to do with Communism or the Soviet Union became increasingly inconceivable. Alan Wolfe writes that following Rusk's theoretical contributions to the Cold War, ". . . every conflict in the world, regardless of how far from home, would be seen as a supreme test of American resolve in the face of communist aggression." The result of such a way of thinking was nearly disastrous: "In the hostile world atmosphere that was the logical result of his 'get tough' stance, Kennedy acted belligerently in Berlin (contributing to the construction of a wall that he was unable to remove), upped the U.S. commitment in Southeast Asia with consequences that would prove disastrous for the United States, and eschewed diplomacy over missiles in Cuba for a confrontation that left the whole world breathless with fear. Within two years, Kennedy had faced more foreign policy 'crises' than faced Eisenhower in all eight of his presidential years."[23]

Alan Wolfe believes that the "folly" of his anti-Soviet hostility came home to John Kennedy shortly before his death. Wolfe refers to the "unusually reasonable" Kennedy speech of June 10, 1963 at American University. In this speech a new accent was placed upon cooperation with the Soviets. Kennedy also was effective subsequently in getting a test-ban treaty through the Senate. Rising U.S. involvement in Vietnam began to absorb the nation's attention, and owing to the growing unpopularity of that situation a foundation slowly began to form in support of detente.

Richard Nixon's success in obtaining approval of the SALT I treaty was an important part of detente. Another important aspect of detente was the political theory of Henry Kissinger, which is characteristic of the Yalta stance: "Kissinger, schooled in the Germanic tradition of political theory, understood that power is inherently conservative. Leaders of countries (and of organizations), he believed, try to protect their privileged position and are inherently suspicious of any challenges to their authority. From this point of view, Kissinger quickly recognized that, whatever their respective ideologies, the U.S. and the Soviet Union were both powerful states that would operate as conservative forces in the world. Both had an interest in protecting themselves from challenges, whether (of concern to the Americans) from other capitalistic countries like Germany, or (of concern to the Russians) from other socialist countries like China, or (of concern to both) from instability in the Third World. Kissinger argued that although there were many possible centers of power in the Third World, the U.S. and the Soviet Union together were so overwhelmingly powerful militarily that they could insure 'stability.' Rather than worrying about Soviet intentions —which in Kissinger's view just 'confuse(s) the debate' — the U.S. should 'discipline power so that it bears a rational relationship to the objectives likely to be in dispute.' While willing to bring up the Soviet threat for domestic purposes, Kissinger was not fixated on it."[24]

The "fairly dramatic" military budget decreases (as a percentage of GNP), and the reduction in shows of military force during this time, make the Nixon years a valley in hostile U.S. perceptions of the Soviet Union. "Without a sharply negative view of an enemy, it is difficult to justify an activist foreign policy."[25]

The period from 1976 to the present seems to Wolfe to be another peak in anti-Soviet hostility. President Carter sought to find a middle way between an alarmist and a benign-appearing stance toward the Soviets. Thus the defense budget increased considerably, but SALT II talks, troop reduction plans in Europe, and restraint in Iran and Africa all characterized the Democratic presidency. This balance was lost, however, at the moment of the announcement that Russian troops were stationed in Cuba.

Surveying the entire post-World War II Cold War history, Alan Wolfe says, "The real issue is not whether the Soviets become more aggressive, but whether the U.S. decides to view them as more aggressive (and vice versa)." Wolfe continues, "What needs to be explained then is why, when the evidence is always ambiguous, the most negative perceptions (of the Soviet Union) develop at the time they do."[26]

The Dominance of the Most Negative Anti-Soviet Views

The first answer to Wolfe's question of why the most negative views of Soviet intentions prevail in the U.S. is that "similar political conditions" in this country help to make this occur. Wolfe writes: "First, a new president, generally a Democrat, assumes office. During this time, the right wing organizes itself around the notion of a Soviet threat, a politically safe issue for them since they are out of power and need not concern themselves with putting new policies into effect. Pressure from the right makes the newly installed president vulnerable. If there was equally strong pressure from the left, in favor of programs oriented toward greater equality and a foreign policy permitting smaller defense budgets, the new president would not be forced to lean rightwards. But without a strong left, Democratic presidents invariably adopt a more aggressive foreign policy as a way of protecting their political base. This also gives them the appearance of being bold and decisive, which cuts down some of the need to adopt aggressive domestic programs — ones that would antagonize big business and conservative interest groups. For all these reasons, the structure of domestic political alignments and coalitions comes to have as much to do with an increase in hostile perceptions of Soviet power as any actions taken by the Soviet Union."[27]

According to Wolfe, Truman's election prospects in 1946 turned upon his choosing correctly between continuing the leftist program of Roosevelt's New Deal and trying to co-opt the growing conservatism articulated by the right. His attempts to hold the broadest possible range of support led to the formation of the coalition known as "Cold War liberalism." Wolfe defines this as a combination of ". . . New Deal attachment to the welfare state with strong support for a cold war foreign policy." The coalition contained interests from "business, labor, intellectuals, and the military."[28] The force holding this coalition together was fear of the Soviet Union. A high military budget functioned in this coalition to spur economic growth by large government outlays; also, exactly by allocating funds in military technology areas the budget seemed pleasing to conservative and business interests on the right.

Moreover, military spending in the West and South enabled interests in those regions to feel vested in the coalition. A momentous consequence of Democratic co-opting of conservative anti-Communism was that to prove their sincerity and competence in maintaining U.S. military supremacy the Democrats have had a right-leaning bias in foreign affairs. The absence of a strong left to balance the rightist influence further contributes to the Democratic party's inclination along this line. Soviet bellicosity has certainly played a part in the overall process, but not so much as the interplay of domestic political considerations which framed the Cold War liberal coalition.

President Kennedy, in Wolfe's opinion, was faced with a typical dilemma as a Democrat. The Democrats always boasted of "doing something" when their rivals "did nothing." Yet Kennedy's need to do something was tempered by his recognition that his election victory margin was very slim. Hence there was a risk of exercising leadership only to find he had lost effective political power. His way ahead, not surprisingly, lay in challenging an accepted adversary, the Soviet Union. In his inaugural address Kennedy advocated a more powerful air force, construction of nuclear missiles, and building the Polaris submarine. Wolfe writes: "Without anything to fear on the left, Kennedy had to worry only about the right. His belligerency toward the Russians protected that flank. Thus, so long as he kept alive the Soviet threat, Kennedy had a relatively clear field to himself."[29]

Wolfe states that Lyndon Johnson's presidency was characterized by some fine domestic policies, but that exactly these policies caused Johnson to fear a right wing backlash. Because of this fear, Johnson believed he should show his military resolve by invading the Dominican Republic and increasing U.S. commitments in Vietnam. "Had Johnson carried over into foreign policy the lessons of the Great Society, he would have broken the cold war liberal pattern, liberated the Democratic Party from its need to exaggerate the Soviet Threat, and conceivably have become one of the greatest American presidents. Instead he was forced to retire in disgrace."[30]

Concerning Republican administrations during the cold war years, Wolfe states that President Eisenhower's genuine conservatism meant that he did not have to project a rigorous anti-Soviet stance. Nixon was in essentially the same position as Eisenhower, and was free from right wing political attack to work out the policy known as detente. By creating detente, Nixon opened the way for Jimmy Carter to become "the first postwar Democrat that did not *need* the cold war." That is, Carter could simply have followed the detente program legitimated by a man whose anti-Communist position was unquestionable. Instead Carter bargained with cold war militants by supporting the MX and advocating increased military spending.

Alan Wolfe summarizes his view thus far: "The main reason why the Soviet Threat will not go away, even when conditions demand that it should, is because of the absence of a strong left in the United States. Without a left, Democratic presidents have little choice but to turn to the right in foreign policy."[31]

Another factor in anti-Soviet hostility is interservice rivalry. Alan Wolfe: "The most negative perceptions of an external enemy tend to occur when the military services cannot agree on their proper share of the budget and make their differences public."[32] Analyzing the relative balances and imbalances in interservice allocations during the cold war years, and correlating these with variations in anti-Soviet hostility, Wolfe comes to this conclusion concerning a "recurrent pattern": "A new party comes to power; that party then shifts money toward its favorite service; those branches that stand to lose will 'discover' the Soviet threat and issue harrowing warnings about America's future; at this point, presidents back off from confrontation (not wanting to appear weak in the face of an external threat); as they back off, the budget begins to climb, a new equilibrium is established, and the most negative perceptions of the Soviet Union begin to taper off."[33]

Still another aspect of Anti-Soviet hostility is the periodic attempts of U.S. presidents to uphold the authority of their office. A strong presidency has served the U.S. well at certain moments in history; at other times it has seemed advisable to limit the power of the presidency. Alan Wolfe puts the matter this way: "In most cases, the relationship between negative perceptions of the Soviet Union and decisions to preserve presidential power are more the result of a coincidence of interest than they are directly intentional. It tends to be the case that those presidents who are most in need of an active foreign policy in order to hold together their governing coalition are those presidents who accept as essential the need for a strong presidency as a solution to domestic and foreign needs."[34]

Presidents Kennedy and Johnson both believed that an active presidency was needed, and that such a presidency was incompatible with a hypersensitivity to the wishes of the Congress. The Watergate scandal during the Nixon years, coupled with the general skepticism arising from the Vietnam experience, undermined the strength of the executive office. The popularity of a president, hence the power of his office, increases during a foreign crisis. Exaggerated views of the Soviet Threat have tended to go hand-in-hand with a strengthened presidency.

Another factor that conditions U.S. perceptions of Soviet intentions is the coherence of domestic policy coalitions ("Negative perceptions of Soviet intentions increase when existing foreign policy coalitions are in disarray and when new coalitions seek to push foreign policy in a new direction.")[35] Still another variable is federal stimulation of the economy by politically safe outlays (preeminently outlays for military purposes).

Wolfe ends his study with this challenge: "A massive peace campaign could take heart from the kinds of issues addressed in this report. I have tried to show how, time after time, elites that possessed extremely unpopular ideas — such as a strong executive, an expensive public sector, an inflationary program, an emphasis on large-scale production, and a demand for domestic sacrifice to stabilize the world economy —have managed to stifle the strong opposition to their vision by manipulating the Soviet threat. The task, then, is to try to take off the husk of the Soviet threat, which does have mass appeal, so that the kernel of an undemocratic and monopolistic economic program, which does not, will be revealed."[36]

In this section an attempt has been made to understand how various intellectual and political leaders in the United States have tended to view the Soviets, and why. To understand the basis of U.S. perceptions and portrayals of the Soviet threat is essential to an informed and rational appraisal of the nuclear arms race. It may be essential to the survival of human life as we have known it.

1. Norman Podhoretz, *The Present Danger.* New York: Simon & Schuster. ©1980 by Norman Podhoretz.

2. Quoted in Podhoretz, p. 13.

3. Podhoretz, p. 31.

4. Podhoretz, p. 40.

5. Quoted in Podhoretz, p. 53.

6. Podhoretz, p. 58.

7. Podhoretz, p. 66.

8. Podhoretz, p. 88.

9. Podhoretz, p. 81.

10. Podhoretz, p. 93.

11. Podhoretz, p. 100.

12. Quoted in Podhoretz, p. 101.

13. George F. Kennan, "A Modest Proposal." Reprinted with permission from *The New York Review of Books,* 28:12. July 16, 1981. p. 14. ©1981 Nyrev, Inc. Kennan's speech also appears in modified form in *The Los Angeles Times* as "On the Nuclear Standoff and Its Insanity." (Sunday, May 24, 1981.)

14. Kennan, *ibid.,* p. 16.

15. Kennan, *ibid.,* p. 16.

16. Alan Wolfe, *The Rise and Fall of the "Soviet Threat": Domestic Sources of the Cold War Consensus.* Washington, D.C.: The Institute of Policy Studies. 1979. (94 pp.)

17. Wolfe, p. 2.

18. Wolfe, p. 5.

19. Wolfe, p. 6.

20. Kaiser, p. 460.

21. Wolfe, p. 17.

22. Wolfe, p. 19.

23. Wolfe, p. 19.

24. Wolfe, p. 24.

25. Wolfe, p. 25.

26. Wolfe, p. 31f.

27. Wolfe, p. 33.

28. Wolfe, p. 34.

29. Wolfe, p. 38.

30. Wolfe, p. 38.

31. Wolfe, p. 42.

32. Wolfe, p. 52.

33. Wolfe, p. 61.

34. Wolfe, p. 47.

35. Wolfe, p. 74.

36. Wolfe, p. 87.

DISCUSSION QUESTIONS
CHAPTER FOUR:
U.S. SECURITY STRATEGIES

1. Describe the "Riga" and "Yalta" views of Norman Podhoretz and George Kennan.

2. As between Podhoretz and Kennan, which major themes, issues, or points do you find most persuasive?

3. Which of the above views seem most compatible with the life and teachings of Christ and the teachings of the church? Why?

4. What is Alan Wolfe's major point concerning U.S. views of the Soviet Threat? Do you agree with Wolfe? Why or why not?

5. Divide into small groups. Imagine that you hold first the view of Podhoretz, then Kennan, then Wolfe.

How do you feel in each posture?

What attitudes or spiritual dispositions are conveyed or nourished by each?

How would each spiritual disposition affect your life with your family, your friends, in your work?

How would each spiritual disposition influence your experience of the liturgy — prayer, confession of sin, Bible reading, communion with God and your neighbor?

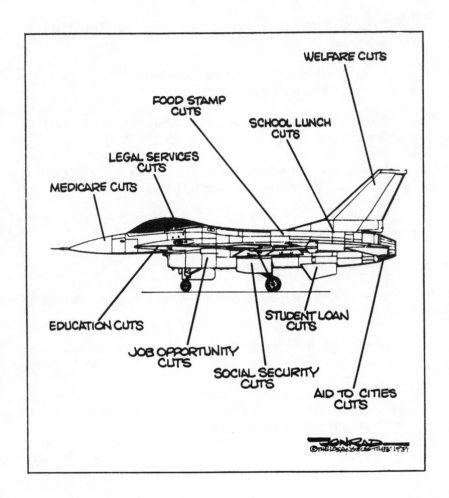

5.

MILITARISM, THE CITIES, AND THE POOR

"Heavenly Father, in your Word you have given us a vision of that holy City to which the nations of the world bring their glory: Behold and visit, we pray, the cities of the earth. Renew the ties of mutual regard which form our civic life. Send us honest and able leaders. Enable us to eliminate poverty, prejudice, and oppression, that peace may prevail with righteousness, and justice with order, and that men and women from different cultures and with different talents may find with one another the fulfillment of their humanity; through Jesus Christ our Lord."

The Book of Common Prayer, p. 825

Cities have long symbolized the best and the worst of which we are capable. The Paris and London of Charles Dickens, the Jerusalem, Nineveh, Bethlehem, and Rome of the Bible — all these signify the fears and hopes that motivate and sustain us.

Today the city's name still compels our imagination. Calcutta, Belfast, Teheran all evince sober images in the minds of most Americans. But Florence, Vienna, Athens, and Copenhagen suggest images of a more positive sort.

The Collect speaks of the "ties of mutual regard which form our civic life." Without such regard there is no basis of mutual trust, no foundation for genuine human community. How close are we in the United States to the "vision of that holy city?"

The Lord God saw our need and had pity. In giving that costliest gift of himself, God came to us right through death itself. Therefore we live.

Consider the cities.

Shall we, too, give to them, as God has given to us?

*   *   *

LAUNCHING PAD

MILITARISM, THE CITIES, AND THE POOR

A Congressional Budget Office report shows the Reagan administration proposing a military budget authority of $180 billion for 1981 and $226.3 billion for 1982.[1] The proposed Reagan military outlays for 1981 are $158.6 billion, rising to $336 billion in 1986, for a six-year total military spending of $1.89 trillion, according to the Center for Defense Information.[2]

Since World War II the idea has persisted that large military expenditures are good for the economy and therefore good for low-income persons. This notion is probably rooted in the memory of a major economic depression that ended with a world war, massive military spending, major arms industry development, widespread industrial employment, and the absorption of millions of unemployed men into the armed forces.

More recent experience, however, raises doubts about the validity of the military spending equals strong economy equation. Economists, social scientists, media observers, human rights advocates, and others have overwhelmingly testified to the economic and social costs of the Indochina War of the 1960s and early 1970s. These analysts have confirmed the earlier opinion of Martin Luther King, Jr., who said, "The Great Society has been shot down on the battlefields of Vietnam."[3] So also Howard University's Faustine Jones, who wrote in the April 1981 *Daedalus:* "The Vietnam War brought an end to this expanded social concern; many insisted that 'guns and butter' could not be secured simultaneously. Domestic programs designed to improve the life chances of minorities were given a lower priority as 'butter' gave way to 'guns,' and as domestic issues generally receded."[4]

Why did the Second World War seem so beneficial for the U.S. economy, and the Vietnam War so hurtful? The most persuasive single explanation is that taxes were used to support World War II, and the Korean War as well, whereas President Johnson did not raise taxes in the Vietnam era and thus deferred that war's costs into the distant future. Indeed, the deferred costs of the Vietnam War are thought to be a part of the current economic predicament. Our present purpose, however, is not to perform a detailed economic and historical analysis, but to make the point that wars and preparations for war are costly to society. The idea that huge military spending is economically good is understandable, but it is also highly dubious when carefully examined.

Since the Episcopal Urban Caucus is vitally concerned about the decay of our nation's cities, and about the consequences of this process for the inhabitants of our cities, a consideration is here given to a few of the predominant aspects of deteriorating urban life, and certain impacts of large military spending.

The Central City

A growing number of persons from all sectors of society have become aware of the growing urban crisis. The breakdown in urban services and institutions, the rise in crime, fear, unemployment, overcrowded housing, drug traffic, and the like are accepted by millions of Americans as simple facts of urban life.[5] People who can manage to leave cities frequently do.

Perhaps the most devastated segments of the U.S. population are the racial minorities trapped in urban poverty. Certainly it is this group with whom the Episcopal Urban Caucus is urgently concerned. Professor Douglas Glasgow of Howard University writes of the hopelessness and despair of young black urban poor, a black underclass, whom he characterizes as "undereducated, jobless, without salable skills or the social credentials to gain access to mainstream life."[6] Citing U.S. Census Bureau reports, Glasgow shows the widening gap in black versus white unemployment; he reports the persistence of poverty and immobility among several generations of blacks and the chronic hopelessness of menial jobs that open to no lasting or upward path to greater opportunity. The dead-end nature of whatever jobs can be found constitutes the primary cause of hopeless feelings as blacks develop a keen sense that the mainstream economy is closed to them. Many blacks find little reason to feel invested in, and therefore committed to, the larger society. Why should people excluded from meaningful participation in a society feel a sincere commitment to the welfare of that society?

To put the question, of course, is to discover the answer. What is needed is a massive infusion of goods, services, and mainly meaningful job opportunities into the cities for the urban poor.

The cities are fraught with tension. Anyone who has sat in the lobby of a social service agency or a large public hospital knows intuitively that to seek charity is both degrading and demoralizing. Anyone who has visited a public housing project senses immediately the emotional costs to the inhabitants of compressing large numbers of people into crowded living areas. Anyone who has visited a city jail has seen the disproportionately large numbers of poor and race minority people imprisoned there. Anyone who has had to apply to anonymous bureaucrats for food, shelter, clothing, and health care — for the self, for the spouse, for the parent, for the children — knows the psychological devastation of

70

living under this kind of constant dependency.

The cities are neglected partly because society's movers and shakers have largely abandoned them. White flight from the cities — especially the central city — and from the city's schools, rising costs of rent and services (frequently paid to persons living in the suburbs) and the apparent indifference or fecklessness of city officials all suggest to the urban poor that racial and class discrimination are real. This perception is not alleviated by attempts in the mainstream sector to blame the victims for their misery.

Do we need the reminder that the race factor is one of the most obvious and vicious in the interplay of forces which brutalize the inner city poor? Despite the sometimes fashionable disclaimers in the mainstream sector that race discrimination is not *intended*, the *effects* of racism are real, and they are considerable, as Douglas Glasgow and numerous others have shown.[7] Though no one claims responsibility or intent, people still end up in segregated patterns of schools, houses, health care facilities, and jobs. This severely diminishes the freedom of choice and overall quality of life for blacks, Mexican-Americans, Puerto Ricans and American Indians — all of whom comprise our nation's largest minority groups.

Jobs: The First Priority

In terms that apply for all the urban poor, Douglas Glasgow concludes *The Black Underclass* with these words, "First and foremost, young blacks need employment that provides not only the important experience of work but also a livable income." Glasgow refutes the vicious myth that poor people prefer not to work, and shows the constant cycle of defeat, rejection, menial and meaningless labor, and the crushing consequences of the same for one's self-esteem. He emphasizes that, ". . . no amount of social rehabilitation, community participation, or motivational programs will substitute for being able to earn a way with self-respect."[8]

It seems reasonable, then, to ask: What is the effect of large military spending upon jobs? What kinds of jobs are created, and what kinds lost? What would happen if some of the money now spent by the military were spent in the civilian sector?

Economist Marion Anderson's 1978 study demonstrated that hundreds of thousands of jobs were lost due to that year's $78 billion in military spending.[9] For every additional $1 billion in military spending, another 11,600 jobs were lost. The reason for these losses is that with money in the civilian population, people are able to buy goods (a car, a radio, furniture, clothes) or services (take a vacation, travel, etc.). Surely the people who receive Defense Department money spend it on goods and services. But when an increasing percentage of the available money in the economy is spent by soldiers in Germany, or by military procurement offices for missiles to be placed in holes in North Dakota, there is less and less money available for goods and services. Consequently, there are fewer and fewer jobs for people who manufacture those goods or deliver those services.

Using data by Yale economist Bruce Russett, Anderson showed that $78 billion spent by the military costs 3,253,000 jobs in civilian industries and services. Of this number, 1,560,000 jobs are lost in such service areas as auto and airline mechanics, baggage handlers, and clerks; 1,011,000 jobs are lost in state and local government; 476,000 jobs are lost in construction, and 663,000 jobs are lost in metal working, transportation equipment, and machinery producing industries.

Statistics from the Department of Labor show that 1 billion dollars supports only 41,000 civilians in Defense Department jobs whereas the same amount of money could support 115,000 jobs in education, 95,000 jobs in health, welfare, and sanitation, and 76,000 jobs in non-durable consumption goods.[10] In short, carrying on a high-technology arms race makes work for the highly skilled, not for the unskilled, and certainly not for the underclass.

The evidence mounts. A study by the prestigious Chase Econometrics Associates determined that $17 billion proposed in 1975 to be spent on the B-1 bomber would eventually cost 30,000 jobs that could otherwise be created if the $17 billion were returned to the public as a tax cut. More, the proposed B-1 program could cost 70,000 jobs that could otherwise be created if the $17 billion were committed for a major public housing program. The principal reason for the high number of jobs lost, according to Chase, is that relatively fewer workers are employed in the high-skill, high-technology military manufacturing sector than would be employed in the manufacture of public housing or other civilian consumer items.[11] Unfortunately a sincere effort to reverse the staggering unemployment problems in our central cities requires precise targeting upon the unemployed underclass; this group will not be benefited by the creation of high technology jobs in the military sector.

A well-known study by economist R. H. Bezdek of the U.S. Energy Research and Development Administration compares the foreseeable results of a 30% *decrease* in Defense Department spending with a corresponding *increase* in health, education, welfare and environmental programs. Bezdek's finding is that in such a case 2.1 million persons would be added to the employment rolls. However, by supposing a 30% *increase* in military spending, and an equivalent *decrease* in human services programs, Bezdek forecast a drop in overall employment by 1.3 million. (As with the Chase study, Bezdek assumed that reductions in military spending were accompanied by equivalent tax cuts or government expenditures in the civilian sector.)[12]

Certainly more studies need to be done to demonstrate the connection between increased military spending and high unemployment rates. Yet the work done to date is highly suggestive that more jobs could be created, and made available to the urban poor, if government funds went more into civilian endeavors and less into military.

Other Costs of Militarism to the Urban Poor: Inflation, Regional Imbalances, and Decaying Civilian Industry

Inflation is a direct result of large military spending, among other causes. A chief reason for this is that enormous military consumption of industrial materials (steel, chemical products, and the like) tends to make these materials scarce. When certain items are scarce, their cost rises. Another reason for military-induced inflation is the addition of large sums of money to society (in the form of salaries to military employees), coupled with the removal from society of products that are socially useless (submarines, tanks, missiles, etc.), and the removal from society of certain useful services (scientific research, health care personnel and facilities, and the like). With more money being made available for fewer and fewer goods and services, the amount of money spent on the available goods and services rises and prices increase (inflation). Still another reason for military-induced inflation is that high wages to military scientists and engineers means that civilian industries must raise wages to compete with the military for competent employees. Cost-plus military contracting, which appears especially on contracts involving a great deal of research and development work, is yet another cause of inflation since profits to military contractors are made *after* all costs are paid by the government. That is, the guarantee that costs will be covered removes the contractor's incentive to keep costs as low as possible.[13]

Another effect of military spending is that tax money is taken from the whole of the public but is spent more lavishly by the military in some areas than in others. According to a recent study by Dr. James R. Anderson of Employment Research Associates,[14] 305 U.S. Congressional Districts each lose an *average* of $170,000,000 each year in taxes for military spending, but 103 Districts each receive more money than they lose in such taxes. This is due to the commitment of large amounts of tax revenue within districts containing major military contractors. Some cities suffer. Anderson shows, for example, that $880,000,000 is drained for Pentagon spending each year from Cleveland. If only two weeks' worth of this money were retained, Cleveland's debts would be paid. Other cities that suffer are New York, which loses $4,410,000,000 to the

Pentagon, Chicago, which loses $3,327,000,000, Detroit $1,482,000,000, Newark $914,000,000, Miami $672,000,000, Pittsburgh $599,000,000, Atlanta $342,000,000, and Philadelphia $46,000,000. Some cities gain. Washington leads with $3,139,000,000 gained yearly by Pentagon spending, followed by San Diego, $1,565,000,000, St. Louis $1,545,000,000, L.A.-Long Beach $1,449,000,000, San Jose $1,239,000,000, and Boston $1,009,000,000. The money that leaves cities is obviously unavailable to rebuild schools or hospitals, pay teachers or nurses, provide recreation or youth services, and the like.

The steady decay of U.S. civilian industry, and an erosion of the ability of U.S. industries to compete with foreign industry is due in large part to enormous military spending, sprawling into an increasing amount of the overall economy. The deterioration of plant, machines, and equipment means an inferiority in goods, the purchase by Americans of higher quality foreign goods, the closure of U.S. plants, and the consequent loss of jobs in this country. Foreign goods begin to replace American goods. Workers lose jobs. This condition worsens with the growing numbers of imported cars, television sets, clothes, cameras, shoes, and other items. How is this understandable in terms of our growing U.S. military expenditures?

First, much of the brightest U.S. scientific and engineering expertise is channeled into military research; therefore it is unavailable to help in the development of higher-quality and lower-cost civilian goods. In Germany and Japan, in contrast to the U.S., large percentages of the brightest research talent is employed in civilian industry. University of Texas economist Lloyd Dumas estimates that from one-third to one-half the total number of U.S. scientists and engineers are employed in military research and development.[15] This occurs because of high salaries, ample resources, research opportunities, the prestige of much military work, and because the military sector is where the work is.

Second the commitment of large amounts of capital required for upgrading industrial capacity for producing civilian goods is diverted into the military. This condition in the United States contrasts with the situation in Germany and Japan, where in 1977 only $252. per capita was spent on the German military and only $47. on the Japanese military. In 1977 $441. per capita was spent in the United States on the military.[16] It should not seem mysterious that with more money thus available for civilian industrial development in Germany and Japan, high quality imports from those countries are flowing into the U.S. at an increasing rate. And, of course, the inability of U.S. goods to be sold in the stores leads to a reduction in their manufacture, which leads to layoffs, and unemployment. Columbia University economist Seymour Melman's most conservative estimate is that in recent years over *3,500,000* U.S. jobs have been lost due to U.S. capital investment overseas and the impact of military spending upon the U.S. economy. Melman's upper range estimate is that from 7,000,000 to 9,000,000 U.S. jobs have recently been lost for the same reasons.[17] The shocking nature of unemployment is conveyed by the fact that each percentage point in the unemployment rate stands for 1,000,000 persons, if we assume a labor force of 100,000,000 persons.

The Cost of Militarism: Human Services

There is no assurance that a dollar spent by the military would otherwise have been spent on human services. However, it is true that the 1982 military budget *increase* of $35 billion is almost exactly the amount of money *cut* from social programs. And it is fair to evaluate military spending in terms of what is lost in human services. Such was the approach taken by U.S. Representatives in the Congressional Black Caucus, which saw a direct connection between military spending increases and human services cuts. They state, "We do not support (Reagan's) trillion dollar increase in the defense budget over the next ten years, nor do we believe that the cost is justified in light of its effect on the funding available for those federal programs which address human needs."[18]

One need not be in favor of the frustration and dependency-inducing effects of many welfare programs to see the urgent need for ameliorating the awful ravages of persistent poverty. Nor need we favor an uncritical acceptance of the old welfare state approach to social problems, as if the New Deal in its various forms is the only sensible social policy to be imagined. There are, after all, millions of Americans who mean to do right by poor people. Our hearts, our imaginations, and our money need to be applied to new solutions to old problems. No matter what social policies we do decide upon, however, it remains true that the *worst* effects of poverty could be mitigated by transferring only a small percentage of monies from the military budget to human services programs. Unfortunately the seven "safety net" programs designed to spare the "truly needy" (Social Security retirement and survivors' benefits, Medicare, veterans' compensations and pensions, Supplemental Security Income, free school lunches, Head Start, and summer jobs for youth) do *not* in fact serve the poor in a significant way. This is because 60% of the 25 million Americans with incomes below the poverty line receive no benefits from these programs.

Instead, the programs that *are* under current administration attack (Medicaid, food stamps, public and subsidized housing, the Comprehensive Employment Training Act, Social Security, Child Nutrition Act, Aid to Families with Dependent Children, the Community Services Administration, and the Legal Services Corporation) *all* serve poor people in substantial numbers.

Medicaid, for instance, has guaranteed at least minimal health care to blind or disabled persons, mothers and children on public assistance, children in foster care, and low-income elderly. Food stamps have guaranteed that low-income families have at least a chance for a healthy diet. The housing program has enabled low and moderate-income people to find relatively decent housing in a shrinking housing market. CETA currently employs over 300,000 low-income workers in public service jobs. Social Security has frequently been the only retirement hope for poor people, and sometimes their only avenue to Medicaid. Child nutrition programs in schools, day care centers, and health care agencies have frequently provided the only nutritious meal received by poor children. AFDC is a barebones public assistance program supporting poor children and their mothers at the deepest levels of poverty. (The Children's Defense Fund has documented that 70% of public assistance recipients are children, and that out of every 10 mothers receiving welfare, 4 are working or seeking work, 3 are caring for preschool children, 1 is disabled, and the other 2 are over 45 with no work experience.)[19] The Community Services Administration operates self-help programs in the poorest neighborhoods in our country. The Legal Services Corporation funds local programs which provide legal services in numerous civil matters directly affecting poor people. All these have been drastically cut in the 1982 Fiscal Year budget.

Of the services not being cut outright, many are being prepared for combining into a lump sum, "block grant" to the States. But 25% of current (1981) allocations for these programs is being cut at the federal level. Moreover, there are no longer requirements that the States target the funds for the especially needy, or indeed that states match federal funds or even maintain their present levels of funding. The programs thus affected are social services under Title XX of the Social Security Act, Title XX day care services, foster care, child abuse prevention and treatment, adoption assistance, developmental disabilities, runaway and homeless children's homes, and rehabilitation services.

The fullest meaning of these human services cuts may be seen against the background of enormous, and increasing, military spending. Perhaps even more startling is to use the background of military *waste*. To give but a few examples, the cost *overrun,* to 1981, on the Navy's current destroyer, frigate, and submarine programs is $42,000,000,000; the cost *overruns,* to 1981, on the Navy's Trident and the Air Force's F-16 programs are $33,000,000,000; the cost *overrun,* to 1981, on the Army's heavy tank (XM-1) program is $13,000,000,000; the cost *overrun,* to 1981, on the Navy's F-18 aircraft program is $26,400,000,000; and the cost *overrun,* to 1981, on the Army's UH-60 helicopter program is $47,700,000,000.[20]

Economics, Fairness, and Christian Morality

The life and teachings of Jesus, and the teachings of the church, have expressed at least the following moral principles:

1. All women, men, and children are of equal value since all are equally precious to God;
2. the valuation of women, men, and children primarily upon the basis of race, income level, age, sex, or nationality is immoral from a Christian point of view;
3. human beings are entitled to the possibility of a productive life, a stake in their society's future, and freedom from degradation based upon economic, racial, age, or gender discrimination;
4. social structures and human attitudes that thwart human possibilities and thereby diminish human life are immoral from a Christian point of view, as are persons who perpetuate them;
5. the God revealed in the Bible is especially concerned about the welfare of persons least advantaged in society — the poor, race minorities, the elderly, and children; and,
6. as followers of the Biblical God and of Jesus of Nazareth, Christians have a special obligation to be advocates for the least advantaged in society.

From the perspective of these principles, and of the overall Biblical story and the history of Christian moral theology, the current economic priorities in the United States appear to be significantly distorted. What then should we do?

Conversion

A spiritual conversion in the hearts of the people will, if genuine, lead to a conversion in the way their lives are lived. "By their fruits you shall know them." What is implied in a conversion from a more militaristic to a less militaristic economy?

Of utmost importance is the recognition that past military spending cuts for which little or no planning occurred were hurtful to workers — especially to women, unskilled labor, those over 45, and the generally less educated. Where diligent planning efforts were made, however, plants were successfully converted from military to civilian production.

Political action may be taken to encourage economic conversion to a non-military economy. In 1978, for example, Democrat George

McGovern and Republican Charles Mathias filed a Senate bill, and Ted Weiss a House bill, which provided that, 1) each industrial plant working on a Pentagon contract, and each military base, would establish a committee of management and employees to plan for a non-military use of that facility; 2) the federal government would create a federal economic conversion commission to plan new civilian capital outlays, job retraining programs, and the development of new markets; 3) each conversion plan would contain protection for all affected employees, guaranteeing incomes at 90% of present levels, health insurance, and moving costs to other job locations.

Federal resources to aid conversion exist in the form of the Defense Department's Office of Economic Adjustment (OEA). The OEA has gone into communities facing a reduction in military spending and organized labor leaders for conversion planning. Its successes occurred when new businesses were created and new facilities purchased with the help of local lending institutions, state economic development agencies, or such federal agencies as the Small Business Administration or the Commerce Department's Economic Development Administration (EDA). The EDA in particular has been helpful in a number of communities, whose experiences are usefully described in official government publications.[21]

The economic areas in which civilian industries could be developed are well known. Philip Webre's *Jobs to People-Planning for Conversion to New Industries* shows that an investment of $7.7 billion annually in improving the nation's railroads would create 164,000 new jobs yearly for the next 15 years; $3.1 billion invested annually for the next 15 years in mass transit would create 192,000 new jobs yearly; $1.4 million invested yearly for 12 years in resource recovery (trash and garbage) systems would generate 40,000 new jobs each year; and $2.1 billion invested annually for 7 years in solar energy development would create 71,000 new jobs each year.[22] The continuing creation of new jobs occurs because "direct" jobs are created within a given industry, as well as "indirect" jobs in industries and services peripheral to the primary industry.

Stockholders can encourage the diversification into civilian industries of firms now heavily dependent upon (and therefore highly vulnerable to changes in) military spending. Corporate planning can be initiated immediately to develop civilian jobs, retrain workers, help in relocation assistance, and the like. As with most challenges, there has been not so much a lack of information or resources as a lack of resolve.

The expected criticism that one has not "shown a better way" seems empty in the discussion of converting from a terribly costly military economy to a healthy civilian economy. The willingness to do what clearly must be done is the rub and thus one believes that the spiritual energy of the churches will be decisive in opening the way to a productive and hopeful life for all people.

The vision of a new heaven and a new earth fires the imaginations of people who have been captured by God's spirit. The challenge of building a truly holy city — of blighted streets made habitable for children, of generous goodwill all around — stands in shocking contrast to the grim construction of nuclear weapons. Where except in the community of God's gracious spirit will be found the zeal to build for love, joy and peace?

1. Congressional Budget Office, *An Analysis of President Reagan's Budget Revisions for Fiscal Year 1982.* Washington, D.C., March 1981. p. 73.

2. A budget authority is the overall amount of money the government may spend in the present and in succeeding years. For example, budget authority allows present planning for future weapons development. Outlays, on the other hand, are money amounts actually spent within a given fiscal year, typically for salaries, direct purchases, retirement pensions, operations and maintenance functions, and the like.

3. Martin Luther King, Jr., Sermon at Riverside Church, New York City, April 4, 1967.

4. Faustine C. Jones, "External Crosscurrents and Internal Diversity: An Assessment of Black Progress, 1960-1980." Reprinted by permission of *Daedalus,* Journal of the American Academy of Arts and Sciences (Vol. 110, No. 2, Spring 1981. p. 76F.)

5. The Harvard-M.I.T. Joint Center for Urban Studies has produced *The Prospective City,* edited by Arthur P. Solomon (Cambridge: M.I.T. Press. 1980.), to give but one example of a vast body of literature concerning urban problems.

6. Douglas G. Glasgow, *The Black Underclass: Poverty, Unemployment and Entrapment of Ghetto Youth.* New York: Vintage Books. 1981. p. vii.

7. See Glasgow, *passim.* See also Thomas Pettigrew, "Race & Class in the 1980s: An Interactive View," *Daedalus* 110:2. Spring 1981. pp. 242ff. Among other things, Pettigrew shows that blacks are concentrated today in the nation's largest cities. He notes, for example, that there are more blacks living in the New York City area than in any southern state. Moreover, in such high-black areas as New York City, Detroit, Philadelphia, Cleveland and Newark, the unemployment rate for minorities has sometimes reached 40%.

8. Glasgow, *ibid.,* p. 173.

9. Reported in Marion Anderson, *The Impact of Military Spending on the Machinists' Union.* Washington: International Association of Machinists. January 1979. 16 pp.

10. U.S. Department of Labor, Bureau of Labor Statistics, *Factbook for Estimating the Manpower Needs of Federal Programs.* Bulletin 1832. Washington 1975.

11. Chase Econometric Associates, *Economic Impact of the B-1 Program on the U.S. Economy and Comparative Case Studies.* Cynwyd, PA: Chase Associates. 1975.

12. R. H. Bezedek, "The 1980 Economic Impact - Regional and Occupational - of Compensated Shifts in Defense Spending," *Journal of Regional Science.* 15. 1975. pp. 183-198.

13. A September 30, 1978 *Systems Acquisitions Report, Quarterly Update,* by the U.S. General Accounting Office, showed a $57 billion waste in 55 major Pentagon projects, due to "cost plus," bad management, poor planning and other factors. This cost the average American family $1,140.00.

14. James R. Anderson, *The Impact of the Pentagon Tax on U.S. Congressional Districts.* Lansing, Michigan: Employment Research Associates. 1979.

15. Lloyd J. Dumas, "Why Buying Guns Raises the Price of Butter," *Christianity and Crisis.* Nov. 27, 1978. pp. 284-286.

16. John Kenneth Galbraith, "The Economy of the Arms Race -and After," *East/West Outlook.* 4:2. May-June 1981. p. 2.

17. Seymour Melman, "Inflation & Unemployment as Products of War Economy," *Bulletin of Peace Proposals.* 9:4 1979. pp. 359-374.

18. Congressional Black Caucus, *Alternative Budget Summary.* Washington, D.C. 1981. 4 pp.

19. Marian Wright Edelman, "Suffer the Little Ones," *Sojourners.* July 1981. p. 18.

20. Seymour Melman, "Looting the Means to Production," *The New York Times.* July 26, 1981. p. 23EY.

21. For further study see Thomas P. Ruane, *Federal Responses to Economic Crises: The Case of Economic Adjustment.* Washington: Department of Defense. 1977.

22. Webre's study is reported in Marion Anderson, *The Impact of Military Spending on the Machinists' Union.* Washington: International Association of Machinists. February 1979. pp. 9-11.

DISCUSSION QUESTIONS
CHAPTER FIVE:
MILITARISM, THE CITIES,
AND THE POOR

1. What does "guns or butter" mean?

2. What shape are our cities in? If you live in a major city, would you prefer to leave if you could? If you live in a suburb, would you prefer to move into the city if you could?

3. Have you visited a large urban public housing project? What kinds of feelings do you have concerning life "in the projects"? What would it be like to live in public housing? Would you choose to live there if alternative housing were available?

4. How would you describe urban schools? If you were a child, would you prefer to attend these schools or alternative schools? Why do the children who attend urban schools attend them?

5. What would it be like to support a family by working in a factory as a racial minority person?

6. Have you ever applied for public assistance? If not, what do you think it would feel like?

7. How does the arms race create jobs for the relatively well-educated, but cost comparatively more jobs for the less well-educated?

8. What are the major aspects of military spending that affect inflation?

9. How does the decay of civilian industry affect working people and the U.S. economy in general? How does military spending contribute to this decay?

10. Discuss: (A) taking $35 billion from its present location in the civilian economy and reallocating it in other areas of the civilian economy is a worthwhile risk to take;

(B) taking $35 billion from the civilian economy and adding it to military spending helps the civilian economy;

(C) taking any major sum of money from the civilian economy should be done only after the poor are carefully protected.

11. Do you think that conversion from a more militaristic to a less militaristic economy is possible?

12. Do you think that conversion from a more militaristic to a less militaristic spirit is possible?

13. Do you think that any kind of conversion is possible?

14. Which population group(s) in the inner cities suffer the most from the arms race and urban decay?

15. Do you believe that the fruits of the Holy Spirit include a life committed to peace in the world and peace in the city?

16. Do you think the Holy Spirit helps us when we need help?

6.

CHRISTIAN PERSPECTIVES UPON WAR

"We have made a great advance in technology without a corresponding advance in moral sense. We are capable of unbinding the forces which lie at the heart of creation and of destroying our civilization . . . It is vital that we see modern weapons of war for what they are — evidence of madness."

> The Archbishop of Canterbury,
> Washington, D.C., 1981

Archbishop Runcie speaks of a "moral sense." So have others of diverse and conflicting views. So also do thoughtful and compassionate persons who use the language of morality ("should," "ought," "right," "wrong," "good," "bad") in recommending different and sometimes contradictory courses of action. A conscientious person is correct in wondering how to choose between different notions of right and wrong, good and bad.

How shall we have at least a sense of which moral principles or recommendations are truly fitting, appropriate, for us? Here is where the figure and teachings of Jesus come together with the overall witness of the Bible and the Church's teachings; and by the enlivening presence of God's Holy Spirit, we are helped.

The term "ethics" derives from the root word "ethos." We are rooted in the Christian ethos, and this gives us our basic orientation to life. Included in our orientation is the conviction that Jesus is lord of all, and that justice, righteousness, and peace are both promised to us and required of us.

The context, or ethos, from which we view the nuclear arms race is defined by such terms as those given above. In all its aspects the nuclear arms race takes on its moral coloration under the light of Christ's life, and in the light of his justice, his righteousness, and his peace.

There is no moral relativism ("what's right for you may not be right for me"). There is first of all the Christ. In his light some things are right and other things wrong. He is the center of our ethos, our ethics. From this ethical starting point, what now about the morality of the nuclear arms race?

*   *   *

DONNA THE DOVE

CHRISTIAN PERSPECTIVES UPON WAR

Christians have had two millenia to reflect upon their moral obligations in times of war and preparations for war. One should not be surprised that a variety of opinions have emerged during that time. Some Christians have taken fairly "rule-oriented" positions, such as that the example and teachings of Jesus make participation in any war impossible for Christians. Others have based their views upon the nature of the war with which they have been confronted; they say something like, "I would have fought the Nazis in 1941, but I would not conscientiously have fought in the Dominican Republic in 1965."

The point is usually granted by thoughtful women and men that somehow the Christian tradition ought to be connected with one's best appraisal of the current world situation; and in a spirit of prayer and openness to Christ's presence a decision should be made toward the most fitting action.

What follows is a brief description of the major historical types of thinking about war: the crusade, the just war, and pacifism. Then an attempt is made to characterize the nature of war in the nuclear era. Finally the Christian categories are evaluated from the perspective of the present nuclear reality. The conclusion is that a crusade ethic is very difficult to support on Christian grounds in the nuclear era; the traditional just war criteria presuppose a non-nuclear world and therefore seem ill-fitted to our present reality; and pacifism, in the sense of active peacemaking, seems most prudent in a world subject to enormous destructive force.

The Crusade

We can see some of the origins of the crusade in the "Holy War" of the Old Testament. The holy war idea achieved its greatest prominence in the time of Israel's judges, before 1000 b.c.e. Its basis apparently was the covenant loyalty between the Lord and his people, which meant on the human side that the people were to trust absolutely in God - not in their arms. Later, during the monarchy period, Israel's kings became more pragmatic and modified the holy war idea. For offensive wars they sometimes used mercenaries, but generally they put their trust more in diplomacy and negotiation than had their forebears. International treaties were employed to buttress the nation's security.

The holy war idea underwent yet another modification in the era of the major prophets. The prophets looked Upon Israel's wars as a means of

God's punishment, either of the gentiles or against Israel herself. The last major holy war waged in Biblical times was the battle of Megiddo, 609 b.c.e., in which King Josiah was killed and his army crushed by Neco of Egypt. At this point the idea that one people could wage a holy war in the name of the God of all people suffered a decisive defeat.

When Israel was carried into exile, the holy war was seen primarily as a revolutionary struggle against the dominant power. The Maccabean revolt by Jewish nationalists later against the Syrian occupation forces, and the two Jewish wars of national liberation against Rome in the Christian era, are examples of the holy war motif. The early Christians spiritualized the holy war altogether, making it essentially a cosmic struggle between Christ and the adversary, with Christ being triumphant.

The crusade itself arose during the 11th Century. Initially its purpose was to bring order to a suspicious and hostile Europe, but quickly the crusade was turned upon the Islamic Turkish infidels. To wage war upon non-Christians was seen as a righteous endeavor. In addressing the Council of Clermont in 1095, Pope Urban II bade Europeans to stop fighting amongst themselves and instead, "Start upon the road to the Holy Sepulchre to wrest that land from the wicked race and subject it to yourselves." Part of the difficulty with Urban's exhortation, and with the crusade spirit, is that it contains little encouragement to restraint or to establish a humane peace.

The Just War

The just war theory was first elaborated in a systematic way by St. Augustine, Bishop of Hippo in North Africa. Augustine was well-trained in Greek thought and drew mainly upon Plato, Artistotle and then Cicero, rather than upon the life or teachings of Jesus, to develop a response to the problem of a church threatened by the barbarians. He believed that the excesses of war could be avoided, and a war be fought as "just," if four conditions were met: 1) the war was intended to uphold justice and establish peace; 2) the war was fought with a loving disposition (Augustine apparently differentiated rather starkly the disposition of one's inner spirit and one's outward actions); 3) the war must be duly authorized by the ruler; 4) the war must be conducted in a just way, that is without excessive violence, vengeance, looting, etc.

Augustine's just war theory was a significant change from the predominantly pacifist inclination of the early church. The Emperor Constantine's recognition of Christianity as the official religion of the Roman Empire, in the 4th Century, led to a considerable increase in the number of Christians in the Roman army. Such figures as Bishop

Eusebius of Caesarea and Bishop Ambrose of Milan also nourished a climate in which pacifism began to give way to just war thinking.

The crusades became the dominant Christian war ethic in the Middle Ages, but with the rise of the European independent city states in the 16th Century, the just war motif resurfaced. During the Reformation period, both Protestants and Catholics used the theory for themselves and against each other. Martin Luther, as Augustine, conceived of war as an aspect of the police power of a government. Calvin espoused the theory, but some of his successors, like others before and since, tended to depart from its restraints in practice.

In its current form the just war theory is the result not only of Augustine's thought, but of the work of Thomas Aquinas and Francisco di Vitoria in the medieval period, the Jesuit Francisco Suarez during the Counter-Reformation, and Hugo Grotius in the 17th Century. The theory which was employed to justify both World Wars, now contains six elements: 1) the just war must be declared by a legitmate authority; 2) the cause must be just, aimed at establishing peace — which typically rules out "wars of aggression"; 3) the war must be a last resort — all attempts at diplomacy and negotiation having been attempted and having failed; 4) the principle of proportionality must be employed — meaning that the good ends of the war must always outweigh the evil means used to attain them; 5) the war must hold a probability of success —otherwise it entails pointless, therefore unjustifiable, destruction; 6) all possible moderation should be used in the war's conduct.

A Christian may morally participate in a war that qualifies as just by meeting *all* the criteria specified above. Moreover, all these criteria must be met through the duration of the war; otherwise the Christian must not continue his participation in the war.

Pacifism

Pacificism today has moved beyond its earlier connotation in the negative sense of excluding the self from the hard struggles, by a simplistic appeal to principle. Pacifism today is more and more conceived in the broader sense of active, courageous, even sacrificial peacemaking. Pacifists point out that just war theories have been used to support any wars that people wanted to fight and that therefore the theory is meaningless in practice. They have noted that the Catholic bishops in Germany refused even to condemn Hitler on the basis of the just war theory. What are the origins of pacifism, and how has pacifism developed in Christian history?

Jesus himself seems to have practiced non-violence, and non-resistance to evil as well, since he apparently used no force against the political authorities of his time. His order to Peter to put away the sword, and his submission to Pilate's authority are the two chief manifestations of this inclination. His sometimes quoted statement that he came not to bring peace but a sword (Matthew 10:34) does not in its context convey an intention to arm people; rather it indicates Jesus's belief that people should cut themselves free of all that would restrain them from faithful service in God's Kingdom.

The general tenor of Jesus's life, his teachings (especially as concentrated in the Sermon on the Mount, Matthew 5-7), the witness of the various New Testament writers, and the testimony of several early church theologians (notably Tertullian, Origen, and Justin Martyr) all support the pacifist-peacemaking function as a cornerstone of the Christian foundation.

Pacifists have held that Christian love for the enemy is not due to sentimental feelings or even pragmatic tactics; it is due instead to the recognition that one's enemy is loved by God and that Christians should love what God loves. Another major tenet of pacifism is that one's Christian identity is more important than one's national identity and that therefore Christian values should be more determinative of conduct than national laws or policies.

The notion of being "born again" means to a Pacifist that one is born in a new worldwide family in which all become sisters and brothers to each other, one in Christ, though they come from many nations and tongues. The one who has been born anew knows the love of Christ which overcomes fears, which breaks down the walls that divide, whether between East and West, male and female, slave and free, Jew and Greek, American and Russian.

Pacifist influence waned after Christianity became the official religion of the Roman empire in the 4th century. At this time many joined the church and many churchmen were or became Roman soldiers in the legions. Pacifism declined further during the crusades and during the ascendancy of just war thinking. Yet it emerged from time to time, as with St. Benedict in 6th century Italy, St. Francis in 13th century Italy, and with Ignatius Loyola in Spain, Erasmus in Holland, and Sir Thomas Moore in England — all in the 16th Century. The Pacifist spirit also arose in such Protestant groups as the Quakers, Mennonites and Brethren. In the present time there has been a resurgence of pacifism, as a growing number of persons think of themselves as being at least minimally pacifist with regard to nuclear weapons.

Christian Ethics in the Nuclear Era

It seems fair to say that at least two factors have operated through the church's history as it has tried to understand its faith. One factor is the guiding influence of the Holy Spirit, conveyed primarily through the scriptures and tradition of the church. Another factor is a lively discernment of the quality of the time and place to which we have come. To lean too heavily upon the first factor runs us the risk of being merely antiquarian; to lean too heavily on the second factor puts us in danger of losing our specifically Christian self-understanding. The task before us is to recognize clearly the reality of our present condition in the world and, with a vision shaped by our Christian heritage, to discern how we ought to live responsibly under the lordship of Christ.

One might stipulate without too much disagreement that the present world situation was structured in a new way beginning in 1945 — the year of the atomic bomb. The first wartime use of that bomb on August 6, 1945 (the Transfiguration on the Christian calendar) marked the beginning of an era in which it was possible to unleash destruction suddenly and on an unprecedented scale. Never before, or since, has the end of one period of history and the beginning of another been so precisely fixed as at 8:15 a.m. on August 6, 1945.

Albert Einstein recognized the historical significance of the atomic bomb when he remarked that the bomb had changed everything but our way of thinking. The changes now require our conscious attention so that our thinking as Christians is responsive to the truth concerning our predicament. The following comprise the major components of the nuclear reality before us:

1. A few nations possess the power to destroy hundreds of millions of persons within hours or a few days.
2. Other nations, a steadily growing number, possess the means to start a nuclear war.
3. Certain factors, such as the speed with which nuclear weapons are conveyed and the treaty obligations between nations, make possible the rapid escalation of limited nuclear wars into world wars.
4. The destructive force of a nuclear weapon is so great and so persistent that even when aimed at a military target a nuclear weapon threatens large numbers of civilian lives. The distinction between combatant and innocent noncombatant is eroded. The traditional analogy of war to police work, whereby the military exists primarily to defend the citizenry, is no longer apt. Formerly war was conceived as the clash of two military forces, each trying to break through the enemy's lines to threaten his civilian population. Nuclear weapons in effect place everyone, soldiers and civilians, on the front lines by making everyone vulnerable to sudden destruction.

5. Massive radiation released by nuclear weapons predisposes all affected human life to future health defects. The future, sometimes unpredictable, implications of radiation effects means that the definition of "casualties" has changed drastically.
6. In the event of "full scale" nuclear war, widespread and perhaps irreversible damage would change the ecosystem of the planet. The destruction of large portions of plant and animal life, changes in the earth's protective ozone layer, and countless other effects might lead to a condition in which life on earth would hardly be recognizable to any humans that might survive.

If the foregoing is a fair characterization of the implications of nuclear war, it seems reasonable to test the major types of Christian ethical thought within such a framework of understanding. To borrow from the language of ethics, what kinds of obligations, rights, values, and commitments ought we have as followers of the Lord Jesus in this kind of world? If this is the world that has changed, how can our thinking change so as to be appropriately realistic *and* faithful?

First, it might be argued that either the U.S. or the Soviet Union, or both countries, have opposed each other in a spirit of crusade. Such an argument would be based upon the perception that the obliteration of life on so large a scale as is entailed in a nuclear was is simply incompatible with restraint and a humane peace. That a major nuclear war would finally lead, too, to mutual forgiveness between the warring nations seems difficult to imagine. The bellicose nature of the crusading spirit seems ill-suited to the nuclear era, wherein the stakes are so high, the destruction of life so horrible to consider. For Christians it seems difficult to imagine Jesus of Nazareth himself leading a crusade or desiring that his disciples participate in one.

Second, the present era, with its nuclear characteristics, seems to be a different kind of reality than that presupposed by the just war theory. The quality of nuclear weapons overwhelms the concepts of conventional warfare upon which just war thinking is based. The basic problem is that to describe a globally destructive nuclear war as just in its purpose, moderate in its conduct, promising of "success," and employing means proportionate to its end, seems absurd. Indeed, to think of a nuclear war as just might suggest that we have forgotten what words really mean. Moreover it is difficult to imagine either that Jesus of Nazareth wants a nuclear war for any reason, or that he would want us to employ the amount of cynicism necessary to name such a war as "just" from a Christian point of view.

Third, pacifism, understood in the active sense of peacemaking, seems increasingly to be the Christian response to war that most fits the post-

1945 reality. The statement of Martin Luther King that, ". . . the choice is between nonviolence or nonexistence" appears to summarize things succinctly for more and more people. Jesus's statement that the Father's love means even the hairs of the head are numbered, is very difficult to reconcile with Christian participation in preparations for nuclear war. Perhaps the bottom line is that we are unable to conceive of Jesus "nuking" anybody. Since this seems so, the *strategy* of peacemaking entails the setting of clear and achievable goals, and the persistent determination to pursue them incrementally. Step-by-step movement, based upon careful study and informed by a mature faith, is the mode of evangelical witness to Christ's peace today.

The purpose of a just war theory has been to show how Christians can defend a just society; yet there is no defense for any society from war in the nuclear era. The most appropriate defense is peacemaking. The presence of nuclear weapons means that the greatest enemy of the U.S. is not the U.S.S.R. or vice versa; the greatest enemy of both nations is nuclear war itself. Theories that intend to justify a war are our enemy; theories that intend to justify peacmaking are our friend. Such is the manner in which our way of thinking itself is changing in the nuclear era.

The unprecedented death and destruction entailed in a nuclear war is characteristic of an apocalyptic time. Nuclear weapons are more indiscriminate in their killing than were Hitler's gas chambers. In an apocalyptic time, things tend to simplify: Is the nuclear war good? Is it right? A Christian who sees the complexity of forces, the ambiguity of all things, nevertheless begins to simplify without becoming simplistic.

From a Christian point of view: Is nuclear war good? Is it right? In an apocalyptic time it seems easier and more truthful to say, simply, "No." To say "No" to nuclear war does not mean that Christians have finished with nuclear war; it means that they have begun to work for peace, begun actively to be peacemakers.

Christian peacemaking rests upon the ethical principles that life is good, that the creation is good, that each individual is precious to God, that all of us are part of one human family, and that room always must be made between persons for love, forgiveness, and reconciliation. From the perspective built upon these principles, peacemaking entails both the building up of human community *and* the tearing down of militarism, understood as the precipitous resort to war as a means to solve international problems.

In an apocalyptic time, salient commitments to peacemaking are both altruistic and self-interested, both idealistic and supremely realistic. Moreover, we have this on excellent authority, "the peacemakers are the blessed ones; they shall be called the children of God."

DISCUSSION QUESTIONS
CHAPTER SIX:
CHRISTIAN PERSPECTIVES
UPON WAR

1. What are the three major attitudes taken toward war by the church during its 2,000-year existence?

2. Name some historical events that appear to express or explain each major attitude.

3. Do the characteristics of war in the nuclear era make one or more of the three attitudes more appropriate than the other(s)? Why?

4. It has been argued elsewhere that one might be a "nuclear pacifist," without being an "absolute pacifist." Do you think the distinction between these two terms is valid? Why or why not?

5. Apply the just war criteria to a nuclear war. Are they able to justify it? Why or why not?

6. Is the spirit of crusade discernable in anti-Soviet feelings within the U.S.? If yes, how does this spirit accord with the Christian ethos?

7.
PLATFORM AND STRATEGIES

A Platform

What is a concrete aim of intelligent peacemakers in an imperfect world? What constitutes both a faithful and a realistic "platform" to which thoughtful Christians can commit themselves today? In general terms a slowing, stopping, and ultimate reversing of the nuclear arms race is needed. But precise program objectives ought to be identified so that purposeful action may be undertaken. The Episcopal Urban Caucus, meeting in February, 1981, recommended the following objectives to the Episcopal Church:

1. The United States government should renounce the first use of nuclear weapons;
2. The United States and the Soviet Union should adopt an immediate mutual freeze on all further testing, production, and deployment of nuclear weapons and of missiles and new aircraft designed primarily to deliver nuclear weapons;
3. The United States government should redirect national resources to civilian technology and human need, especially in our cities.

The third objective above requires our acknowledgment that the nuclear arms race and the urban plight at some level are independent situations; yet at another level it remains profoundly true that resources committed for nuclear weapons purposes are in fact unavailable for improving the urban environment. To force a widespread recognition of the military spending/urban plight connection is an urgent objective for the church today. This connection ought to be forced onto the national agenda at the highest priority level.

The U.S.-Soviet nuclear weapons freeze also warrants our close attention since the freeze is currently the most widespread and rapidly growing popular effort to control the arms race. For example, the September/October 1981 Interfaith Center *Newsletter* reported that a summertime Gallup Poll showed that 72% of Americans favor a bilateral nuclear weapons freeze, with 20% opposed and 8% undecided.

The freeze statement is here reprinted in its entirety, with its three-sentence proposal and extensive supporting statements:

CALL TO HALT
THE NUCLEAR ARMS RACE
Proposal for a Mutual
U.S.-Soviet Nuclear-Weapon Freeze

To improve national and international security, the United States and the Soviet Union should stop the nuclear arms race. Specifically, they should adopt a mutual freeze on the testing, production and deployment of nuclear weapons and of missiles and new aircraft designed primarily to deliver nuclear weapons. This is an essential, verifiable first step toward lessening the risk of nuclear war and reducing the nuclear arsenals.

The horror of a nuclear holocaust is universally acknowledged. Today, the United States and the Soviet Union possess 50,000 nuclear weapons. In half an hour, a fraction of these weapons can destroy all cities in the northern hemisphere. Yet over the next decade, the U.S.A and U.S.S.R. plan to build over 20,000 more nuclear warheads, along with a new generation of nuclear missiles and aircraft.

The weapon programs of the next decade, if not stopped, will pull the nuclear tripwire tighter. Counterforce and other "nuclear warfighting" systems will improve the ability of the U.S.A. and U.S.S.R. to attack the opponent's nuclear forces and other military targets. This will increase the pressure on both sides to use their nuclear weapons in a crisis, rather than risk losing them in a first strike.

Such developments will increase hairtrigger readiness for a massive nuclear exchange at a time when economic difficulties, political dissension, revolution and competition for energy supplies may be rising worldwide. At the same time, more countries may acquire nuclear weapons. Unless we change this combination of trends, the danger of nuclear war will be greater in the late 1980s and 1990s than ever before.

Rather than permit this dangerous future to evolve, the United States and the Soviet Union should stop the nuclear arms race.

A freeze on nuclear missiles and aircraft can be verified by existing national means. A total freeze can be verified more easily than the complex SALT I and II agreements. The freeze on warhead production could be verified by the Safeguards of the International Atomic Energy Agency. Stopping the production of nuclear weapons and weapon-grade material and applying the Safeguards to U.S. and Soviet nuclear programs would increase the incentive of other countries to adhere to the Nonproliferation Treaty, renouncing acquisition of their own nuclear weapons, and to accept the same Safeguards.

A freeze would hold constant the existing nuclear parity between the United States and the Soviet Union. By precluding production of counterforce weaponry on either side, it would eliminate excuses for further arming on both sides. Later, following the immediate adoption of the freeze, its terms should be negotiated into the more durable form of a treaty.

A nuclear-weapon freeze, accompanied by government-aided conversion of nuclear industries, would save at least $100 billion each in U.S. and Soviet military spending (at today's prices) in 1981-1990. This would reduce inflation. The savings could be applied to balance the budget, reduce taxes, improve services, subsidize renewable energy, or increase aid to poverty-stricken third world regions. By shifting personnel to more labor-intensive civilian jobs, a nuclear-weapon freeze would also raise employment.

Stopping the U.S.-Soviet nuclear arms race is the single most useful step that can be taken now to reduce the likelihood of nuclear war and to prevent the spread of nuclear weapons to more countries. This step is a necessary prelude to creating international conditions in which:

— further steps can be taken toward a stable, peaceful international order;

— the threat of first use of nuclear weaponry can be ended;

— the freeze can be extended to other nations; and

— the nuclear arsenals on all sides can be drastically redueed or eliminated, making the world truly safe from nuclear destruction.

For list of endorsers, see page 101.

Statement on the
Nuclear-Weapon Freeze Proposal

Scope of the Freeze

(1) Underground nuclear tests should be suspended, pending final agreement on a comprehensive test ban treaty.

(2) There should be a freeze on testing, production and deployment of all missiles and new aircraft which have nuclear weapons as their sole or main payload. This includes:

U.S. Delivery Vehicles	Soviet Delivery Vehicles
In Production:	*In Production:*
Improved Minuteman ICBM	SS-19 ICBM
Trident I SLBM	SS-N-18 SLBM
Air-launched cruise missile (ALCM)	SS-20 IRBM
	Backfire Bomber

In Development:	In Development:
MX ICBM	SS-17, SS-18, SS-19 ICBM
Trident II SLBM	improvements
Long-range ground- and sea-launched cruise	NEW ICBM
missiles (GLCM, SLCM)	New SLBM (SS-N-20)
Pershing II IRBM	
New bomber	

(3) The number of land- and submarine-based launch tubes for nuclear missiles should be frozen. Replacement subs could be built to keep the force constant, but with no net increase in SLBM tubes and no new missiles.

(4) No further MIRVing or other changes to existing missiles or bomber loads would be permitted.

All of the above measures can be verified by existing national means of verification with high confidence.

The following measures cannot be verified nationally with the same confidence, but an effort should be made to include them:

(5) Production of fissionable material (enriched uranium and plutonium) for weapon purposes should be halted.

(6) Production of nuclear weapons (bombs) should be halted.

There are two arguments for attempting to include these somewhat less verifiable steps. First, with a halt to additional and new delivery vehicles, there will be no need for additional bombs. Thus, production of weapon-grade fissionable material and bombs would probably stop in any event. Second, the establishment of a *universal* ban on production of weapon-grade fissionable material and nuclear bombs, verified by international inspection as established now for non-nuclear-weapon states under the Nonproliferation Treaty and the International Atomic Energy Agency, would greatly strengthen that Treaty and improve the prospects for halting the spread of nuclear weapons.

The Agreement to Freeze

The U.S. and Soviet governments should announce a moratorium on all further testing, production and deployment of nuclear weapons and nuclear delivery vehicles, to be verified by national means. The freeze would be followed by negotiations to incorporate the moratorium in a treaty. The negotiations would cover supplementary verification measures, such as IAEA inspections; and possible desirable exceptions from the freeze, such as an occasional confidence test.

This procedure follows the precedent of the 1958-61 nuclear-weapon test moratorium, in which testing was suspended while the U.S.A., U.S.S.R. and U.K. negotiated a partial test ban treaty.

Relation to SALT Negotiations

The bilateral freeze is aimed at being introduced in the early 1980s, as soon as sufficient popular and political support is developed to move the government toward its adoption.

The freeze would prevent dangerous developments in the absence of a SALT treaty. It would preclude exploitation of loopholes in past treaties and, at the same time, satisfy critics who are concerned that the SALT process may not succeed in stopping the arms race.

The freeze does not replace the SALT negotiating process, but should supplement and strengthen it. The freeze could be adopted as a replacement for SALT II or as an immediate follow-on, with the task of putting the moratorium into treaty language the job of SALT III.

The Case for a Nuclear-Weapon Freeze

There are many reasons to support a halt to the nuclear arms race at this time.

Parity — There is widespread agreement that parity exists between U.S. and Soviet nuclear forces at present.

Avoiding "Nuclear Warfighting" Developments —The next generation U.S. and Soviet nuclear weapons improve "nuclear warfighting" capabilities — that is, they improve the ability to knock out the enemy's forces in what is termed a "limited" nuclear exchange. Having such capabilities will undermine the sense of parity, spur further weapon developments and increase the likelihood of nuclear war in a crisis, especially if conflict with conventional weapons has started. It is of overriding importance to stop these developments.

Stopping the MX and New Soviet ICBMs —Specifically, a freeze would prevent the deployment of new and improved Soviet ICBMs, which are expected to render U.S. ICBMs vulnerable to preemptive attack. This would obviate the need for the costly and environmentally-destructive U.S. mobile MX ICBM, with its counterforce capability against Soviet ICBMs. That, in turn, would avoid the pressure for the U.S.S.R. to deploy its own mobile ICBMs in the 1990s.

Stopping the Cruise Missile — The new U.S. cruise missile, just entering production in an air-launched version and still in development in ground- and sea-launched versions, threatens to make negotiated, nationally-verified nuclear arms control far more difficult. Modern, low-flying, terrain-guided cruise missiles are relatively small and cheap and can be deployed in large numbers on virtually any launching platform: not only bombers, but also tactical aircraft, surface ships, tactical submarines, and various ground vehicles. They are easy to conceal and, unlike ICBMs, their numbers cannot be observed from satellites. If the United States continues the development and production of cruise missiles, the U.S.S.R. will be likely to follow suit in 5-10 years, and quantitative limits on the two sides will be impossible to verify. A freeze would preclude this development.

Preserving European Security — A freeze would also prevent a worsening of the nuclear balance in Europe. To date, the U.S.S.R. has replaced less than half of its medium-range nuclear missiles and bombers with the new SS-20 missile and Backfire bomber. The United States is planning to add hundreds of Pershing II and ground-launched cruise missiles to the forward-based nuclear systems in Europe, capable of reaching the U.S.S.R. Negotiations conducted *after* additional Soviet medium-range weapons are deployed are likely to leave Europe with more nuclear arms on both sides and with less security than it has today. It is important to freeze before the Soviet weapons grow to large numbers, increasing pressure for a U.S. response and committing both sides to permanently higher nuclear force levels.

Stopping the Spread of Nuclear Arms — There is a slim chance of stopping the spread of nuclear weapons if the two superpowers stop their major nuclear arms race. The freeze would help the U.S.A. and U.S.S.R. meet their legal and political obligations under the Nonproliferation Treaty. It would make the renunciation of nuclear weapons by other countries somewhat more equitable and politically feasible. In addition, a U.S.-Soviet freeze would encourge a halt in the nuclear weapon programs of other countries which are known or believed to have nuclear weapons or nuclear-weapon technology. These are Britain, France and China, with publicly acknowledged nuclear weapon programs, and India, Israel and South Africa, without acknowledged programs.

Timing — There is a unique opportunity to freeze U.S. and Soviet nuclear arms in the early 1980s. The planned new U.S. and Soviet ICBMs and the U.S. Pershing II and ground-launched cruise missile are not scheduled to enter production until 1982 or later. The Soviets have offered to negotiate the further deployment of their medium-range nuclear forces and submarine-based forces. Given the pressure to respond to new weapons on both sides and the existing nuclear parity, an equally opportune time for a freeze may not recur for many years.

Popular Appeal — Campaigns to stop individual weapon systems are sometimes treated as unilateral disarmament or circumvented by the development of alternative systems. The pros and cons of the SALT II Treaty are too technical for the patience of the average person. In contrast, an effort to stop the development and production of all U.S. and Soviet nuclear weapons is simple, straight-forward, effective and mutual; and for all these reasons it is likely to have great popular appeal.

This is essential for creating the scale of popular support that is needed to make nuclear arms control efforts successful.

Economic Benefits — Although nuclear forces take only a small part of U.S. and Soviet military spending, they do cost some tens of billions of dollars annually. About half of these funds go to existing nuclear forces, while half are budgeted for the testing, production and deployment of new warheads and delivery systems. A nuclear-weapon freeze, accompanied by government-aided conversion of nuclear industries to civilian production, would yield several important economic benefits:

— About $100 billion each (at 1981 prices) would be saved by the United States and the Soviet Union over the period from 1981 to 1990 in unnecessary military spending.

— The savings could be applied to balance the budget; reduce taxes, improve services now being cut back; subsidize home and commercial conversion to safe, renewable energy sources; or increase economic aid to poverty-striken third world regions, thereby defusing some of the tinderboxes of international conflict.

— With the shift of personnel to more labor-intensive civilian jobs, employment would rise. At the same time, the highly inflationary pressure of military spending would be mitigated.

Verification

The comprehensive nature of a total freeze on nuclear weapon testing, production and deployment (and, by implication, development) would facilitate verification.

Long-range bomber and missile production would be proscribed. The letter of assurance attached to the draft SALT II Treaty that the U.S.S.R. will not increase its rate of production of Backfire bombers indicates not only *deployment* but also *production* of the relatively large aircraft and missiles in question can be observed with considerable confidence. While concealed production and stockpiling of aircraft and missiles is theoretically possible, it would be extraordinarily difficult to accomplish with no telltale construction or supply. Any attempt would require the building or modification of plants and the development of new transport lines that are not operational at present. It would also involve high risks of detection and high penalties in worsening relations without offering any significant strategic advantage.

Verification of a ban on *tests* of missiles designed to carry nuclear weapons can be provided with high confidence by existing satellite and other detections systems. Here, too, a comprehensive approach is easier to verify than a partial or limited one.

Verification of aircraft, missile and submarine *deployments,* by specific quantity, is already provided under the terms of the SALT II and SALT I Treaty language. Verifying *no* additional deployments or major modifications will be considerably easier, in fact, than checking compliance with specific numerical ceilings in a continually changing environment.

Verification of a comprehensive nuclear *weapon test* ban, the subject of study and negotiation for many years, has been determined to be possible within the terms of the existing draft comprehensive test ban treaty.

Initiatives Toward the Freeze

Either the United States or the Soviet Union could initiate movement toward the freeze by taking modest, unilateral steps that would: demonstrate its good faith, start movement in the right direction, and make it easier for the other country to take a similar step.

For example, either country could:

1. Undertake a three-month moratorium on nuclear test explosions, to be extended if reciprocated.

2. Stop further deployment, for a specified period, of one new strategic weapon or improvement of an existing weapon.

3. Draw up and publish comprehensive conversion plans for the nuclear facilities and employment that would be affected by a freeze, as a sign of serious commitment to the goal.

Endorsers of a Bilateral
Nuclear-Weapon Freeze (Partial List)

American Friends Service Committee
Richard Barnet, co-Founder
Institute for Policy Studies*

Br. Romard Barthel, Administration
Congregation of the Holy Cross*

Kenneth Boulding, President
American Economic Association*

T. Berry Brazelton, M.D.
Pediatrician

Cambridge Democratic City Council

Catholic, Episcopal, Jewish and Presbyterian Peace Fellowships

Rep. Shirley Chisholm, NY

Church Women United

Clergy and Laity Concerned

Harvey Cox, Theology
Harvard University*

Sr. Vivian M. Coulon, Cong. Superior
Marianites of the Holy Cross
Rep. Ron Dellums, CA

Disarmament Working Group, Coalition for a New Foreign & Military Policy

Freeman Dyson, Physicist
Institute for Advanced Studies*

Richard Falk, International Law
Princeton University*

Bernard Feld, Editor-in-Chief
Bulletin of Atomic Scientists*

Fellowship of Reconciliation

Seymour Maxwell Finger
Former Ambassador to the UN

John Ford, Mayor
Tuskegee, Alabama

Randall Forsberg, Director
Inst. for Defense & Disarm. Studies*

Rabbi Daniel Freelander
Union of American Hebrew Congregations*

John Kenneth Galbraith, Economist

Dan Gaby, President
Keyes-Martin & Co.*

Jerome Grossman, Director
Council for a Livable World*

C. Willard Heckel, former Dean
Rutgers Law School*

Adam Hochschild, Publisher

Wilbur Hogg
Episcopal Bishop of Albany .

Holy Cross Interprovince Justice & Peace Commission

H. George Jacobs, Founder and President
American Polymers*

Robert Johansen, Prsident·
Institute for World Order*

Alan Kay, Businessman

George Kistiakowsky
Former Science Advisor to President

Executive Committee, Leadership Conference of Women Religious

Joel Lebowitz, former President
NY Academy of Sciences*

Carl Marcy, former Staff Director
Senate Foreign Relations Committee*

Peter Matheson, Author of *Snow Leopard*
1979 National Book Award

Mobilization for Survival

Rep. Toby Moffett, CT

Philip Morrison, Book Review Editor
*Scientific American**

Michael Myerson, Director
*U.S. Peace Council**

National Council of Churches

Rep. Richard Ottinger, NY

Pax Christi

Eugene Pickett, President
*Unitarian Universalists Associations**

George Rathjens, Arms expert
*Mass. Institute of Technology**

Rep. Frederick Richmond, NY

Riverside Church Disarmament Program

Rep. Charles Rangel, NY

Rep. Peter Rodino, NJ

Sane

Harris Schrank, Vice-President
*Equitable Life Assurance Society**

Victor Sidel, M.D.
*Physicians for Social Responsibility**

Sisters of Loretto

Sojourners

Office for Church in Society, United Church of Christ-

Rep. Harold Washington, IL

Rep. James Weaver, OR

Rep. Ted Weiss, NY

Robert White, Sec. for Social Witness
*Reformed Church in America**

William Wickersham, Director
*World Federalists Association**

Herman Will
*United Methodist Church**

William Winpisinger, President
*International Assoc. of Machinists**

Rabbi Arnold Wolf
*K.A.M. Isaiah Israel Congregation**

Women's International League for Peace and
Freedom

World Peacemakers

*organizations for identification only

Action Suggestions

1. Make copies of the Call and send them to three friends.
2. Identify three leaders in your community. Send them the Call and follow up by telephone or in person.
3. Get the organizations to which you belong to endorse the Call.
4. Use a petition-format of the Call for a bilateral freeze for house-to-house and large-meeting canvassing and to gather names and funds for local newspaper ads calling for a bilateral nuclear-weapon freeze.
5. Initiate city or town government resolutions, state government resolutions or statewide election referendum questions in support of the freeze.
6. Create a citizens' group to take petitions, resolutions and other expressions of support for a freeze to discuss with your Representative, Senators and Governor. Learn their opinions and work for their support and endorsement of the freeze.

Strategies

Persons who believe that the nuclear arms race ought to be slowed, stopped, then reversed, will recognize the importance of effective action. The following are simple suggestions concerning tasks that local individuals or groups can perform as a means to achieving concrete objectives. Since any strategy will be sensible to the extent that it fits the local situation, the ideas presented here are meant to be suggestive only.

Study. Usually our opinions are no more persuasive than the facts upon which they are based. Therefore a conscientious study of the major aspects of the arms race is essential. The mutual accountability of a group is frequently helpful in holding people to the discipline required for serious and sustained study. Study materials are easily obtained from libraries, diocesan offices, and groups already working on the arms race (see *Consultation and Support,* below).

Organize. People can be gathered together from within the parish, from a number of congregations, and/or from the community at large. Organizing religious persons is frequently accomplished more effectively when the support of clergy, vestry, or social concerns committees is obtained. The support and information exchange that occurs among a network of arms race groups helps to keep vitality and creativity alive in each individual organization.

Educate. Education of those not yet involved in reversing the arms race is essential. Church and community educational endeavors may be carried out by such means as home meetings, public forums, film festivals, displays, advertisement of pertinent T.V. and other media events, workshops, retreats, and the like. A good starting place is the creation of a library of printed and media materials. Training programs can be developed to help people improve communication skills, analyze legislation and legislative processes, practice presentations to political and other leaders, learn organizing techniques, become effective public speakers, and the like.

Lobby. Letters, phone calls, postcards, petitions, and telegrams can be used to reach political figures, business leaders, and others who influence public opinion. A telephone tree is a rapid response mechanism when urgent matters arise. Visits to home offices of elected officials are frequently effective, as are visits to any community leader.

Religious Witness. Prayer is a crucial commitment. Additionally, worship services can be designed around themes which highlight the arms race. Vigils, fasts, retreats, and public liturgical events all can bear witness to the religious basis of concern regarding the nuclear arms race.

Consultation and Support are available to local individuals and groups from any number of sources. On the East Coast the Riverside Church Disarmament Program has had a great deal of experience in dealing with churches concerning the arms race. The Riverside address is 490 Riverside Drive, New York, NY 10027, (212-749-7000). On the West Coast, a resource is the Interfaith Center to Reverse the Arms Race, 132 N. Euclid Avenue, Pasadena CA 91101, (213-449-9430). Still another resource is the Louisville Council for Peacemaking, 1277 Everett Avenue, Louisville, KY 40204. The Arms Race Task Force of the E.U.C. is at 2891 Ticknor Ct., Ann Arbor, MI. 48104. (313) 971-9486. And the Episcopal Peace Fellowship is at Wisconsin and Woodley, N.W., Washington, D.C. 20016. (202) 363-5532.

Worship: The Decisive First Step

Persons who have prayed together, talked and struggled together for several weeks may want to mark the end of their study journey and the beginning of their peacemaking ministry liturgically. Certainly they may want to re-identify themselves and their commitments in the sacramental context where Christ himself is present. To help in that endeavor, a sample Eucharist liturgy is here offered.

A GRAND OLD PATRIOTIC CELEBRATION

Using Rite Two, from *The Book of Common Prayer*

VOLUNTARY   Variations on "America"
                                    — David N. Johnson (contemporary)

PROCLAMATION   *PEOPLE STAND.*

>   Minister: "We hold these truths to be self-evident, that all people are created equal, that they are endowed by their Creator with certain unalienable Rights, that among these are Life, Liberty and the pursuit of Happiness."

>   People: "For the support of this Declaration, with a firm reliance on the Protection of Divine Providence, we mutually pledge to each other our Lives, our Fortunes and our sacred Honor."

>   From the Declaration of Independence, 1776

ENTRANCE   *REMAIN STANDING: EVERYONE SINGS.*

>   O beautiful for spacious skies, for amber waves of grain,
>   For purple mountain majesties above the fruited plain!
>   America! America! God shed His grace on thee,
>   And crown thy good with brotherhood from sea to shining sea.

>   O beautiful for pilgrim feet, whose stern, impassioned stress
>   A thoroughfare for freedom beat across the wilderness!
>   America! America! God mend thine every flaw,
>   Confirm thy soul in self control, thy liberty in law.

O beautiful for heroes proved in liberating strife,
Who more than self their country loved, and mercy
 more than life!
America! America! May God thy gold refine,
Till all success be nobleness, and every gain divine.

O beautiful for patriot dream that sees, beyond the
 years,
Thine alabaster cities gleam, undimmed by human
 tears!
America! America! God shed His grace on thee,
And crown thy good with brotherhood from sea to
 shining sea.
Amen.

— Words by Katharine Lee Bates (1859-1929)
Music by Samuel A. Ward (1847-1903)

COLLECT FOR PURITY   *REMAIN STANDING.*

Minister: Almighty God, to you all hearts are open, all desires
known, and from you no secrets are hid: Cleanse the
thoughts of our hearts by the inspiration of your
Holy Spirit, that we may perfectly love you, and
worthily magnify your holy Name; through Christ
our Lord.

People: Amen.

SUMMARY OF THE LAW

Minister: Jesus said, "The first commandment is this:
Hear, O Israel: The Lord our God is the only Lord.
Love the Lord your God with your heart, with all
your soul, with all your mind, and with all your
strength. The second is this: Love your neighbor as
yourself. There is no other commandment greater
than these."

Mark 12:29-31

108

IN PLACE OF THE GLORIA

REMAIN STANDING:
EVERYONE SINGS.

I'm gonna lay down my sword and shield, down by
the riverside,
Down by the riverside, down by the riverside,
I'm gonna lay down my sword and shield,
Down by the riverside, down by the riverside.

Chorus: I ain't gonna study war no more,
I ain't gonna study war no more,
I ain't gonna study war no more. *(Repeat)*

I'm gonna walk with the Prince of Peace, down by
the riverside,
Down by the riverside, down by the riverside.
I'm gonna walk with the Prince of Peace,
Down by the riverside.

Chorus

I'm gonna shake hands around the world, down by
the riverside,
Down by the riverside, down by the riverside.
I'm gonna shake hands around the world,
Down by the riverside.

Chorus   *(Sung Twice)*

COLLECT

Minister: The Lord be with you.

People: And also with you.

Minister: Let us pray.

REMAIN STANDING.

Minister: Eternal God, in whose perfect kingdom no sword is
and drawn but the sword of righteousness, no strength
People: known but the strength of love: So mightily spread
abroad your Spirit, that all peoples may be gathered

109

under the banner of the Prince of Peace, as children of one Father; to whom be dominion and glory, now and for ever.   Amen.

A PEOPLE OF HOPE COMMITTED TO PEACE   *SEATED.*

(A personal statement by a lay leader of the parish committee to reverse the arms race).

LITURGICAL DANCE   *SEATED.*

FOLLOWING THE DANCE, THE CONGREGATION STANDS AND SINGS:

How many roads must a man walk down
before you call him a man?
Yes 'n' how many seas must a white dove sail
before she sleeps in the sand?
Yes 'n' how many times must the cannon balls fly
before they're forever banned?
The answer, my friend, is blowin' in the wind
The answer is blowin' in the wind.

How many times must a woman look up
before she can see the sky?
Yes 'n' how many ears must one woman have
before she can hear people cry?
Yes 'n' how many deaths will it take till she knows
that too many people have died?
The answer, my friend, is blowin' in the wind
The answer is blowin' in the wind.

How many years can a mountain exist
before it's washed to the sea?
Yes 'n' how many years can some people exist
before they're allowed to be free?
Yes 'n' how many times can a man turn his head
pretending he just doesn't see?
The answer, my friend, is blowin' in the wind
The answer is blowin' in the wind.
The answer, my friend, is blowin' in the wind
The answer is blowin' in the wind.

— Words and music (1962) by Bob Dylan

THE GOSPEL   *REMAIN STANDING.*

Minister: The Holy Gospel of our Lord Jesus Christ according to St. Matthew (5:1-12)

People: Glory to you, Lord Christ.

When Jesus saw the crowds he went up to the hill. There he took his seat, and when his disciples had gathered round him he began to address them. And this is the teaching he gave:

"How blest are those who know their need of God;
   the kingdom of Heaven is theirs.
How blest are the sorrowful;
   they shall find consolation.
How blest are those of a gentle spirit;
   they shall have the earth for their possession.
How blest are those who hunger and thirst to see
   right prevail;
   they shall be satisfied.
How blest are those who show mercy;
   mercy shall be shown to them.
How blest are those whose hearts are pure;
   they shall see God.
How blest are the peacemakers;
   God shall call them his sons.
How blest are those who have suffered persecution
   for the cause of right;
   the kingdom of Heaven is theirs.

How blest are you, when you suffer insults and persecution and every kind of calumny for my sake. Accept it with gladness and exultation, for you have a rich reward in heaven; in the same way they persecuted the prophets before you."

Minister: The Gospel of the Lord.

People: Praise to you, Lord Christ.

111

Mine eyes have seen the glory of the coming of the
Lord;
He is trampling out the vintage where the grapes of
wrath are stored;
He hath loosed the fateful lightning of his terrible
swift sword!
His truth is marching on.

Glory! Glory! Hallelujah!
Glory! Glory! Hallelujah!
Glory! Glory! Hallelujah!
His truth is marching on.

In the beauty of the lilies Christ was born across the
sea,
With a glory in his bosom that transfigures you and
me;
As he died to make all holy, let us live to make all
free!
While God is marching on.

Glory! Glory! Hallelujah!
Glory! Glory! Hallelujah!
Glory! Glory! Hallelujah!
While God is marching on.

Glory! Glory! . . .

SERMON   "Renewing our Commitment to Justice and Peace"
                                                    Minister

PRAYERS OF THE PEOPLE   *STANDING.*

Reader: I hear Him in the wind
              and love is woven into a blanket of peace.
          Because God is in my heart and humanity lies softly
              in my mind
          The glory of His presence is in the blades of grass
              and in the wildflowers we gather.

112

Congregation: Do not lose sight of God.
Hear, O Israel!

Reader: I look into the eyes of men and women
and search for the image of God.
I look into the soul of humanity
and discover God's work.
I remember the holiness of God and
manifest the holiness of humanity.

Congregation: Hear O Israel, says the prophet Moses.
What does it mean to hear?

Reader: People who attend a concert with their minds on
business,
Hear — but do not really hear.

Congregation: People who listen to a speaker's words
and think that someone else is being addresssed,
Hear — but do not really hear.

Reader: People who listen to the words of their friends,
or their wives or husbands or children
and do not catch the note of urgency:
"Notice me, help me, care about me,"
Hear — but do not really hear.

Congregation: People who stifle the sound of their conscience
and tell themselves they have done enough already,
Hear — but do not really hear.

Reader: Do not lose sight of God, reads the scripture.
What does it mean to see God?

Congregation: People who walk amidst birds on a cloudless spring
day
and think only of what they will have for dinner,
See — but do not really see.

Reader: People who watch the news
and think only of how it will affect the stock market,
See — but do not really see.

Congregation: People who read unemployment statistics
and see only numbers
See — but do not really see.

Reader: People who see their fellow men and women in prayer
and do not feel the call to join them,
See — but do not really see,

Congregation: People who look at the mushroom cloud of a nuclear explosion
and listen to the engines of war grinding on yet pretend that
the holocaust will never come,
Do not see — and do not hear.

Reader: We pray that our ability to hear and see will be strengthened.

Congregation: May we hear the music of the world,
and the infant's cry, and the lover's sigh.

May we see in the faces of our friends,
expressions of their pleas and dreams.

Reader: May we hear within ourselves the yearnings for peace
that are struggling for expression and join ourselves
together in a community of resistance
to the threat of nuclear war.

May we see the things in the world that proclaim God's existence.
And may we engage ourselves with them.

Congregation: May we read and hear again the words of old,
"Before you this day are set life and death.
Choose life, that you and your children may live."

THE PEACE

Minister: The peace of the Lord be always with you.

People: And also with you.

Greet one another in the name of the Lord.

AT THE OFFERTORY. *At this point individuals may place personal commitments to work for peace in the offering plate.*

Anthem
SEATED.

Lord, make me an instrument of Thy peace.
　Where there is hatred, let me sow love.
Where there is injury, pardon.
　Where there is doubt, faith.
Where there is despair, hope.
　Where there is darkness, light.
Where there is sadness, joy.
　O, Divine Master, Grant that I may not
so much seek to be consoled as to console;
　To be understood as to understand;
To be loved, as to love;
　For it is in giving that we receive,
It is in pardoning that we are pardoned,
　and it is in dying that we are born to eternal life.

— Music by Sven Lekberg (b. 1899)
Text is the Prayer of St. Francis

FOR THE PRESENTATION   Hymn 141, "America"
STANDING: EVERYONE SINGS.

English, 1740

My country, 'tis of thee,
Sweet land of liberty,
Of thee I sing;
Land where my fathers died,
Land of the pilgrims' pride,
From every mountainside
 Let freedom ring.

Our father's God, to thee,
Author of liberty,
To thee we sing;
Long may our land be bright
With freedom's holy light;
Protect us by thy might,
 Great God, our King.
Amen.

S. F. Smith, 1832

THE GREAT THANKSGIVING   *STANDING.*

Priest: The Lord be with you.

People: And also with you.

Priest: Lift up your hearts.

People: We lift them to the Lord.

Priest: Let us give thanks to the Lord our God.

People: It is right to give him thanks and praise.

Priest: God of all power, Ruler of the Universe, you are worthy of glory and praise.

People: Glory to you for ever and ever.

Priest: At your command all things came to be: the vast expanse of interstellar space, galaxies, suns, the planets in their courses, and this fragile earth, our island home.

People:	By your will they were created and have their being.

Priest:	From the primal elements you brought forth the human race, and blessed us with memory, reason, and skill. You made us the rulers of creation. But we turned against you, and betrayed your trust; and we turned against one another.

People:	Have mercy, Lord, for we are sinners in your sight.

Priest:	Again and again, you called us to return. Through prophets and sages you revealed your righteous Law. And in the fullness of time you sent your only Son, born of a woman, to fulfill your Law, to open for us the way of freedom and peace.

People:	By his blood, he reconciled us. By his wounds, we are healed.

Priest:	And therefore we praise you, joining with the heavenly chorus, with prophets, apostles, and martyrs, and with all those in every generation who have looked to you in hope, to proclaim with them your glory, in their unending hymn:

SANCTUS/BENEDICTUS

Priest and People say:	Holy, holy, holy Lord, God of power and might, heaven and earth are full of your glory. Hosanna in the highest. Blessed is he who comes in the name of the Lord. Hosanna in the highest.

THE CONSECRATION   *KNEELING.*

Priest:	And so, Father, we who have been redeemed by him, and made a new people by water and the Spirit, now bring before you these gifts. Sanctify them by your Holy Spirit to be the Body and Blood of Jesus Christ our Lord.

On the night he was betrayed he took bread, said the

blessing, broke the bread, and gave it to his friends, and said, "Take, eat: This is my Body, which is given for you. Do this for the remembrance of me."

After supper, he took the cup of wine, gave thanks, and said, "Drink this, all of you: This is my Blood of the new Covenant, which is shed for you and for many for the forgiveness of sins. Whenever you drink it, do this for the remembrance of me."

Remembering now his work of redemption, and offering to you this sacrifice of thanksgiving,

People: We celebrate his death and resurrection,
as we await the day of his coming.

Priest: Lord God of our Fathers; God of Abraham, Isaac, and Jacob; God and Father of our Lord Jesus Christ: Open our eyes to see your hand at work in the world about us. Deliver us from the presumption of coming to this Table for solace only, and not for strength; for pardon only, and not for renewal. Let the grace of this Holy Communion make us one body, one spirit in Christ, that we may worthily serve the world in his name.

People: Risen Lord, be known to us in the breaking of the Bread.

Priest: Accept these prayers and praises, Father, through Jesus Christ our great High Priest, to whom, with you and the Holy Spirit, your Church gives honor, glory, and worship, from generation to generation.

People: Amen.

Priest: And now, as our Savior Christ has taught us, we are bold to say,

People: Our Father, who art in heaven,
hallowed be thy Name,
thy kingdom come,

thy will be done,
on earth as it is in heaven.
Give us this day our daily bread.
And forgive us our trespasses,
as we forgive those
who trespass against us.
And lead us not into temptation,
but deliver us from evil..
For thine is the kingdon,
and the power, and the glory,
for ever and ever. Amen.

THE BREAKING OF THE BREAD

A period of silence is kept, during which the Priest breaks the consecrated Bread.

Priest: Alleluia. Christ our Passover is sacrificed for us.

People: Therefore let us keep the feast. Alleluia.

INVITATION

Minister: The Gifts of God for the People of God.

DURING COMMUNION

Everyone sings: Hymn 528, "Melcombe"

S. WEBBE, 1782

O God, of love, O king of peace,
Make wars throughout the world to cease;
The wrath of sinful man restrain,
Give peace, O God, give peace again!

Remember, Lord, thy works of old,
The wonders that our fathers told;
Remember not our sin's dark stain,
Give peace, O God, give peace again!

Whom shall we trust but thee, O Lord?
Where rest but on thy faithful word?
None ever called on thee in vain,
Give peace, O God, give peace again! Amen.

H. W. Baker, 1861

ANTHEM

How beautiful are the feet
of them that preach the gospel of peace,
and bring glad tidings of good things!

— From *Messiah* by G. F. Handel (1685-1759)

H. L. HASSLER, 1601

HYMN

Choir sings: Because we are God's children, wherever we may be,
One union shall unite us forever proud and free.
No tyrant shall defeat us; no nation strike us down.
All who toil shall greet us the whole wide world
around.

Everyone sings: Together as God's children we go forth hand in hand;
Where chimes the bell of Freedom, there is our native
land.
God's children's fears are my fears; yellow, white, or
brown;
God's children's tears are my tears, the whole wide
world around.

Let every voice be thunder; let every heart be strong.
Until all tyrants perish our work shall not be done.
Let not our memories fail us, the lost years shall be
found.

120

Let slavery's chains be broken the whole wide world
around.

— Adaptation and text by Tom Glazer
Musical setting of verse 1 by J.S. Bach (1685-1750)

Everyone sings: We shall overcome, we shall overcome,
We shall overcome some day.
Oh, deep in my heart I do believe
That we shall overcome some day.

We shall all be free, we shall all be free,
We shall all be free some day.
Oh, deep in my heart I do believe
That we shall all be free some day.

We'll walk hand in hand, we'll walk hand in hand,
We'll walk hand in hand some day.
Oh, deep in my heart I do believe
That we'll walk hand in hand some day.

We will live in peace, we will live in peace,
We will live in peace some day.
Oh, deep in my heart I do believe
That we will live in peace some day.

We shall overcome, we shall overcome,
We shall overcome some day.
Oh, deep in my heart I do believe
That we shall overcome some day.

— Text by Zilphia Horton
Music by Frank Hamilton, Guy Carawan,
and Pete Seeger

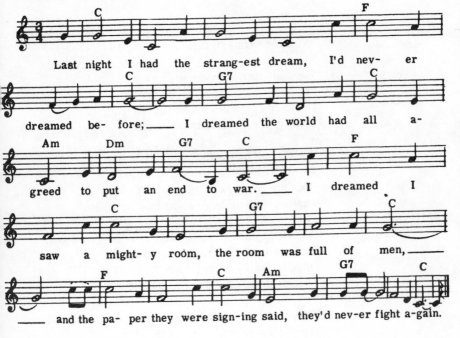

Last night I had the strang-est dream, I'd nev-er dreamed be-fore;___ I dreamed the world had all a-greed to put an end to war.___ I dreamed I saw a might-y room, the room was full of men,___ and the pa-per they were sign-ing said, they'd nev-er fight a-gain.

And when the paper was all signed
And a million copies made
They all joined hands and bowed their heads
And grateful prayers were prayed.

And the people in the streets below
Were dancing round and round,
And swords and guns and uniforms
Were scattered on the ground.

(Repeat first verse)

— Words and music by Ed McCurdy

Everyone sings: Let us break bread together on our knees
Let us break bread together on our knees
When I fall on my knees with my face to the rising
    sun,

122

Oh, Lord, have mercy on me.

Let us drink wine together on our knees
Let us drink wine together on our knees
When I fall on my knees with my face to the rising
    sun,
Oh, Lord, have mercy on me.

Let us praise God together on our knees
Let us praise God together on our knees
When I fall on my knees with my face to the rising
    sun,
Oh, Lord, have mercy on me.

THE PRAYER OF THANKSGIVING   *KNEELING.*

Minister
    and
  People:

Eternal God, Heavenly Father,
    you have graciously accepted us as living members
        of your Son our Savior Jesus Christ,
    and you have fed us with spiritual food
        in the Sacrament of his Body and Blood.
Send us now into the world in peace,
    and grant us strength and courage
    to love and serve you
    with gladness and singleness of heart;
    through Christ our Lord. Amen.

THE BLESSING

HYMN 143, "National Hymn"

G. W. WARREN, 1892

God of our fathers, whose almighty hand
Leads forth in beauty all the starry band
Of shining worlds in splendor through the skies,
Our grateful songs before thy throne arise.

Thy love divine hath led us in the past,
In this free land by thee our lot is cast;
Be thou our ruler, guardian, guide, and stay,
Thy word our law, thy paths our chosen way.

From war's alarms, from deadly pestilence,
Be thy strong arm our ever sure defence;
Thy true religion in our hearts increase,
Thy bounteous goodness nourish us in peace.

Refresh thy people on their toilsome way,
Lead us from night to never-ending day;
Fill all our lives with love and grace divine,
And glory, laud, and praise be ever thine. Amen.

D. C. Roberts, 1876

VOLUNTARY   "America" — Variation VIII
                        — David N. Johnson (contemporary)

INDEX

128